ION

PLATO

ION

WITH INTRODUCTION AND NOTES

by

J. M. MACGREGOR

Cambridge:
at the University Press
1956

CAMBRIDGE UNIVERSITY PRESS
Cambridge, New York, Melbourne, Madrid, Cape Town,
Singapore, São Paulo, Delhi, Mexico City

Cambridge University Press
The Edinburgh Building, Cambridge CB2 8RU, UK

Published in the United States of America by Cambridge University Press, New York

www.cambridge.org
Information on this title: www.cambridge.org/9781107620117

First edition 1912
First published 1912
Reprinted 1956
First paperback edition 2013

A catalogue record for this publication is available from the British Library

ISBN 978-1-107-62011-7 Paperback

CONTENTS

PREFACE

FOR the matter contained in the first two sections of the Introduction acknowledgment is due to the various histories of Greek philosophy, in particular to those of Ritter and Preller and of Zeller, and to the monograph on Plato by the late Professor D. G. Ritchie. The section on the MSS. is based upon the writings of Schanz and Professor J. Burnet, to whom I am also indebted for information concerning the sources from which the various readings are derived. Especial thanks are due to Professor Henry Jackson, who read the Introduction and Notes in the manuscript and added to former kindnesses by forwarding a number of valuable and suggestive comments.

Something should perhaps be added concerning the references given in the Notes to Rutherford's School Greek Grammar. In the criticism of Classical Education during the past few years not a little has been said concerning the futility of the *abstract* teaching of Greek and Latin grammar. Experience has shown a tendency on the part of students to interpret this criticism as absolving them from the necessity of using, or even possessing, a text-book on the grammar of the language which they profess to be studying. It therefore seemed desirable, especially in the case of young students, such as those for whom this edition is intended, to indicate the vital connection between a formal Greek Grammar and the writings of Greek authors.

J. M. M.

Liscard,
   September, 1912.

INTRODUCTION

LIFE OF PLATO.

SEVERAL accounts of the life of Plato have come down to us[1]. These accounts however are all of late date; the statements which they make do not always agree; and they contain much which is obviously fabulous and not a little which appears to be based upon erroneous inferences from Plato's own works[2]. With such material to work upon it is impossible to arrive at certainty. It is true that we have some incidental references which rest upon a better authority, e.g. the statement of Aristotle (*Metaphysics*, I. 6) as to the philosophic doctrines which exercised an influence upon Plato. It is possible also to draw some conclusions with certainty from the philosopher's own writings, e.g. his interest in statesmanship, as evidenced by the *Republic* and the *Laws*. But in the main we have to depend for our knowledge of Plato's life on uncritical and unreliable authorities.

Plato came of an aristocratic family. His father's name is given as Ariston and through his mother, Perictione, he could claim kinship with the great Athenian law-giver, Solon. He was born in the year 427 B.C. at Athens, or, as another account has it, in Aegina, where his father had had land assigned to him under the Athenian military

[1] See Appendix I.

[2] e.g. Plato is said by some to have met the Magi, by others to have failed to do so; he is described as the son of Apollo; his visit to the Magi was perhaps inferred from the mention of Zoroaster in the *First Alcibiades* (121 E, 122 A).

occupation of the island[1]. According to tradition Plato[2] was trained in music by Dracon, a pupil of the famous Damon, in letters by Dionysius and in gymnastics by Ariston of Argos. His prowess, we are told, was exhibited at the great athletic festivals of Greece, at Olympia, Delphi, Nemea and the Isthmus, but the accounts vary and there is probably much exaggeration. As a young man Plato would naturally serve in the army in the last period of the Peloponnesian war. The names of contests, in which he bore a part, are given, but it is chronologically impossible for him to have fought in the well-known battles at Tanagra (456 B.C.) and Delium (424 B.C.). The mention of these engagements would seem to be due to some confusion in the minds of our authorities[3].

In his early days Plato is said to have devoted himself to painting and to poetry. Some verses ascribed to him have come down to us. But later, abandoning these pursuits, he gave himself up entirely to philosophy and burned, so the story runs, a tragedy with which he was about to compete. From Aristotle (*Metaphysics* I. 6) we learn that Plato as a young man came under the influence of the doctrines of Heracleitus—an influence which is strongly marked in some of the Platonic writings. Afterwards he turned his attention to the Pythagorean and Eleatic Schools, while, most important of all, he fell under the spell of the personality and teaching of Socrates. The intimacy between the two philosophers is attested by a passage in Xenophon (*Memorabilia*,

---

[1] The Athenians expelled the Aeginetans from their island and occupied it with cleruchs in 431 B.C.

[2] He is said to have been called after his grandfather Aristocles, but to have received the name Plato because of his broad ($\pi\lambda\alpha\tau\acute{u}s$) shoulders or forehead or, according to others, on account of the breadth of his style.

[3] Antisthenes the Cynic is said, in Diog. Laert. VI. i. 1, to have been present at the battle of Tanagra, and Socrates fought at Delium (Plato, *Symposium*, 221 A).

III. 6. 1), where we are told that Socrates was favourably inclined towards Glaucon, the son of Ariston, for the sake of Charmides, the son of Glaucon, and for the sake of Plato. At the final scene, when Socrates was compelled to drink the hemlock, Plato was not present. But in the *Phaedo* he has described the fortitude and magnanimity of his great teacher on that occasion and has paid tribute to his master in one of the noblest passages in all literature.

The writers of Plato's life all agree in stating that he travelled widely. The desire to bring the Greek thinker into contact with the wisdom of the ancient civilizations of Egypt and the East seems to have led Plato's biographers to infer from passages in his works that he had consorted with the Magi in Phoenicia and the priests in Egypt[1]. Similarly the occurrence of the name of Theodorus of Cyrene, the mathematician, in the *Theaetetus* has perhaps given rise to the statement that Plato himself visited that country. It would appear that after the death of Socrates in 399 B.C. Plato withdrew for a time to Megara. That he visited Sicily on more than one occasion, and probably South Italy as well, seems certain.

According to the tradition Plato first went to Sicily to view the island and witness an eruption of Mount Etna. While there he came in contact with Dionysius, tyrant of Syracuse, who displeased with the philosopher's political views caused him to be sold as a slave. His friends, however, procured his release and a garden was bought for him in the Academy, where he taught his doctrines. When the elder Dionysius died, Plato returned to Sicily hoping to secure from Dionysius, the late tyrant's son and successor, land and citizens wherewith to establish his ideal commonwealth. Failing to obtain these he returned to Athens, but later visited Sicily a third time in order to make peace

---

[1] For the Magi, cf. *sup*. p. ix. n. 2. Plato's biographer treats Socrates' oath in the *Gorgias* (482 B), 'By the dog, the god of the Egyptians,' as evidence of a visit to Egypt.

between his friend, the statesman Dion, and the younger Dionysius. He did not succeed, however, in effecting a reconciliation and coming back to Athens continued his teachings, until he died at an advanced age and was buried in the grove of Academus.

PLATO'S WRITINGS.

In addition to the verses mentioned above there have been handed down as Plato's a collection of letters, a will, and a number of prose works. Of the letters some were rightly regarded as spurious by the Alexandrian critics and modern scholars have been disposed to doubt the genuineness of the rest. The will has perhaps a better title to be considered authentic. It has been observed that it contains no reference to the philosopher's books—a point not likely to be omitted by a forger in a later age. Among the prose works attributed to Plato several of minor importance were clearly not written by him. The spuriousness of some of these was recognized by the scholars of Alexandria.

Almost all the works of Plato are written in the form of dialogues or conversations between several speakers. Among a people of lively intellect and social instincts, who enjoyed moreover a large amount of leisure, it was not unnatural that enquiry should take the form of a discussion and that instruction should be imparted through the medium of conversation. That this was the practice of philosophers in Sicily and Southern Italy in the early years of the fifth century B.C. may be seen from the fragments of the comic poet Epicharmus (flor. circ. 480 B.C.). In more than one passage[1] this writer presents to us in verse, apparently by way of burlesque, philosophic and quasi-philosophic arguments in a manner strongly resembling that afterwards

[1] See Appendix II.

employed in prose by Plato. In particular at Athens Socrates sought for truth rather by questioning individuals and examining their answers than by listening to the formal discourses of professing teachers. By his interrogations Socrates aimed at convicting his interlocutors of obscure and inconsistent thinking and at stimulating them to better methods and renewed effort in the pursuit of knowledge. It was with the same objects in view and in imitation of the conversations of Socrates that the dialogues of Plato were written.

The choice of the dialogue in preference to other literary forms was doubtless due also in great measure to that dramatic instinct which to a very marked degree Plato possessed. A reader of the dialogues can scarcely fail to be struck by the combination of strength and delicacy which the writer exhibits in his powers of characterization[1]. If we may trust the tradition, Plato had in this regard an excellent model. So great, we are told, was the esteem in which he held the mimes of the Sicilian writer Sophron that he slept with them under his pillow. Sophron's writings have unfortunately not been preserved. But if we may judge from Theocritus' fifteenth idyll ('The women at the festival of Adonis'), which is said to be based upon one of Sophron's mimes, his work was marked by an insight into character and by a skill and vigour in its portrayal which may well have excited the admiration of Plato.

Apart from the dramatic interest with which it enables a writer to invest a subject, the use of dialogue possesses several advantages. A literary form which professes to reproduce the conversations of actual life cannot fairly employ, at any rate without explanation, a technical phraseology unintelligible to all but a few special students of a particular science. There is further no need to have recourse again and again to stereotyped formulae in order to

---

[1] On the delineation of character in the *Ion*, vide pp. xix—xxi.

introduce objections to the argument or to furnish additional explanations. The natural pauses and lively interruptions which are used in Plato's dialogues to signalize points of transition compare favourably with such expressions as the ἀπορήσειε δ' ἄν τις of Aristotle (*Nic. Eth.* II. 4). Another advantage of dialogue has been pointed out by Plato himself (*Rep.* 348 A). If, he says, we have a mass of arguments on the one side arrayed against a mass of arguments on the other, we require a jury to decide between them. But if we proceed step by step, testing and establishing each point in the argument before advancing to the next one, we arrive at a conclusion based on a solid foundation and avoid the necessity of having to strike a balance between conflicting opinions.

On the other hand the dialogue may at times become merely formal and the interlocutor pass into little more than a personified πάνυ μὲν οὖν or πῶς γὰρ οὔ; In such passages the dramatic interest naturally tends to disappear. It may also be urged with some force that the language of everyday life cannot provide an adequate medium for the expression of philosophic truth. Thoughts which transcend the range of those which our usual words express require a special, technical terminology. Further, scientific accuracy can ill tolerate the looseness with which our vocabulary is ordinarily employed. Thus it is that Plato finds himself compelled to limit and define the meaning of certain terms which he employs. It must be remembered too that in dialogue it is the author who both asks and answers the questions. He can therefore frame his query in a special manner so as to suggest a particular reply. Thus he has an opportunity, if he so desires, of evading difficulties or at least of passing over them in a plausible fashion.

ANALYSIS OF THE *ION*[1].

The *Ion* is a brief dialogue between Socrates and the rhapsode Ion. The main lesson to be drawn from it is that a mere unreflecting appreciation of poetry must not be confounded with an intelligent and reasoned criticism of it. The argument may be analysed as follows:—

(i) *Introduction* (530 A—D). Ion of Ephesus, a rhapsode, arrives at Athens from Epidaurus where he has secured the first prize at the festival of Asclepius. Socrates meeting him and learning of his success expresses the hope that he may be similarly fortunate at the Panathenaea. He remarks upon the enviable position of the rhapsode who wears a fine costume and occupies himself with the study of the poets generally and Homer in particular in regard both to their language and meaning. For the rhapsode must be acquainted with the poet's meaning, if he is to interpret him to an audience. Ion agrees, declaring that this part of the art is his peculiar excellence ; in fact he deserves to be crowned by admirers of Homer for his services in it.

(ii) *The critic must understand poetry as a whole* (530 D—532 B). Socrates will take an opportunity of hearing Ion some day. At present he will only enquire if Ion confines himself to Homer. Ion replies that this is so, but that he can expound other poets equally well when they say the same things about a subject as Homer. Homer and Hesiod both speak about the art of the seer and Ion confesses that a seer would expound their meaning better than he could, whether what the poets said concerning the art was the same or different[2]. Socrates asks if poets have not a general

---

[1] In the ancient classification of Plato's writings the *Ion* is ranked as a λόγος πειραστικός, *i.e.* a tentative discussion.

[2] This line of argument is developed later in the dialogue, 537 A—540 D.

subject-matter; Ion admits this is so, but says they treat it differently. By 'differently,' he explains, he means 'better and worse.' Socrates enquires if the man who knows when a man speaks well about numbers is the same as he who knows when a man speaks ill. Ion answers that he is the same man, the arithmetician. Similarly it is the same man, the physician, who knows both good food and bad. Knowledge of the 'good' and the 'bad' is found in the same person. Hence the critic of good poetry must also know bad poetry, and we shall not be wrong in declaring Ion's skill to apply to other poets as well as to Homer.

(iii) *The argument is supported by the analogy of other arts* (532 B—533 C). What is the reason then, asks Ion, of his apathy and inattention when other poets are the subject of discussion, and his eagerness and enthusiasm about Homer? Socrates thinks he can guess the reason. He is sure that Ion cannot speak about Homer from art and knowledge. Has Ion ever seen a painter who could only explain the works of Polygnotus and treated all others with indifference? Or a sculptor devoted solely to Theodorus the Samian? Has he ever found a man who could tell what was good and what was bad only in the performance of a single artist, be he a player on the flute or lyre, a singer to the guitar or a rhapsode?

(iv) *The nature of Ion's appreciation of Homer is explained*[1] (533 C—536 D). Ion allows his inability to dispute the argument but reiterates that upon Homer he speaks better than anyone, is never at a loss and receives universal approbation. Socrates replies that this is because he is filled with inspiration by the god. The god's influence is like that of the magnet, which not only attracts iron rings itself but infuses into them a similar power. Like the bacchant, the poet is no longer his own master when he composes, but simply the mouthpiece of the god. This is

[1] The explanation is of course tinged throughout with irony.

shewn by the fact that the several poets compose in several different styles. If a poet knew the art of poetry as a whole, he would be able to write in each and every style. The poet is filled with enthusiasm by the god, the rhapsode by the poet, the audience by the rhapsode, just as an iron ring is endowed with the power of attraction by a magnet, a second ring by the first, a third by the second. One poet is inspired by one Muse, another by another. One rhapsode is fired by one poet, another by another. As worshippers indulge in ecstasies of dance and song only when they hear the strain of the god who possesses them, so it is only when mention is made of Homer that Ion's eloquence finds utterance.

(v) *The application of certain arts to the Homeric poems is indicated* (536 D—539 E). Ion is still doubtful if his praise of Homer springs from inspiration and not from knowledge. Socrates, he thinks, would agree with him, if he were to hear him speaking. Socrates declares he would willingly do so, but asks first which is the part of Homer's subject-matter upon which Ion speaks best. All of it, replies Ion. Homer in many places speaks of special arts, *e.g.* chariot-driving (*Il.* XXIII. 335). Ion admits that here the chariot-driver will judge Homer better than he. Each particular art understands a particular subject-matter and one art differs from another when it deals with a different subject-matter. To understand the same subject-matter we must use the same art, but a different art for a different subject-matter. Therefore a rhapsode cannot understand a passage where Homer speaks of chariot-driving, of mixing a potion (*Il.* XI. 639), of casting a line into the sea (*Il.* XXIV. 80), or of the prophetic art (*Od.* XX. 351 ; *Il.* XII. 200). For these we require the chariot-driver, the physician, the fisherman and the prophet.

(vi) *Where does Ion's art apply?* (539 E—541 D). Which portions then of Homer's writings belong to the rhapsode? All of them, asserts Ion. But he has forgotten his former admission that the art of the rhapsode has a separate subject-matter (537 D) and is therefore a separate art (538 B). Ion then cannot claim the parts of the poems which belong to other arts. Accordingly he qualifies his former 'all' by the addition of 'except what belongs to other arts.' This, he explains, includes 'what it befits a man or woman, a slave or free man, a ruler or subject to say.' But Socrates points out that this becomes the subject-matter of different arts according to the circumstances in which the speaker is placed. It is the sea-captain who knows what a man in command ought to say in a storm, the neatherd who is aware of the proper language for a slave to use when his kine grow restive. Ion maintains that the rhapsode knows how a general should address his troops, and that he knows this in virtue of being a rhapsode, since there is no difference between the arts of the rhapsode and the general. Ion, says Socrates, is the best rhapsode in Greece ; therefore he must be the best general. It is strange then that the Greeks do not employ him. Athens has made other foreigners her generals.

(vii) *Conclusion* (541 E—542 B). Socrates declares that Ion is not acting fairly, if he really can praise Homer from art and knowledge. Ion promised to shew him many fine things which he knew about Homer and has not even explained how his skill applies to the poems, but has evaded the question and turned out at last a general. Yet if Ion's appreciation of Homer is due not to knowledge but to the inspiration of the god, Socrates allows that he has not been treated unjustly. Ion must choose between being considered unjust and being regarded as inspired. He prefers the latter alternative.

THE CHARACTERS OF THE DIALOGUE.

Slight as the dialogue is, the characters of the speakers are vividly presented to the reader by a few graphic touches. Ion's natural vanity has been exaggerated by his recent victory at Epidaurus and he regards with self-satisfaction the coming contest at the Panathenaea[1]. He is flattered by Socrates' reference to the splendid dress and lofty calling of the rhapsode and boastfully maintains his superiority to all other critics and his great services to the study of Homer[2]. So proud is he of his art that he twice makes an attempt to display it to Socrates[3], seizing eagerly on the opportunity for recitation afforded by the other's defective memory[4], and shewing apparently a disinclination to stop once he has begun[5]. He no doubt trusted to produce as powerful an effect as that which usually attended his efforts[6].

But Ion's ignorance is equal to his vanity. In reply to Socrates' questions he at once reveals his inability to conceive the true scope of the art of criticism, imagining that the work of one poet may be studied in complete isolation from that of all others[7]. He cannot clearly distinguish what it is in the poems that forms his peculiar subject-matter but becomes confused and ridiculous when interrogated upon this point[8]. He is an artist unable to indicate his material. Thus in reality he is not a critic at all, but, as Socrates declares, a man inspired with an ecstatic enthusiasm by the genius of Homer, one whose admiration for the poet's work is unbounded, but at the same time unreflecting and unintelligent[9]. And in default of being able to shew where the knowledge to

---

[1] 530 A. [2] 530 C, D. [3] 530 D: 536 D.
[4] 537 A. [5] cf. ἀρκεῖ, 537 B. [6] 535 E.
[7] 531 A. [8] 539 E. [9] 533 D—536 D.

which he lays claim is applicable to Homer, Ion at last, characteristically enough, consents to be regarded as filled with a divine inspiration[1].

Yet this concession is not made without a struggle, for in Ion vanity and ignorance are, as is usually the case, allied with obstinacy. While attracted by the idea of being considered inspired he is yet unwilling to admit his lack of art and knowledge[2]. We find him taking refuge in idle and unfruitful distinctions[3], in an appeal to personal feeling[4], or in simple reiteration of a previous statement[5], when he realizes that he can no longer resist the weight of his opponent's argument. Finally he does not hesitate to set facts at defiance and to fly in the face of all experience[6], in order to avoid the necessity of allowing himself to be mistaken. Yet on the whole Ion was probably not an unpleasant man to meet. He seems to have been a grown-up child ; with the vanity, unreflectiveness and mutinous spirit of childhood; but with its enthusiasm also and no doubt something of its attractiveness.

To Ion Socrates affords an effective foil. His modesty is in striking contrast to the rhapsode's boastfulness and he disclaims for himself the title σοφός[7]. While acknowledging the other's accomplishments and professing his readiness some day to listen to a display of them he endeavours by questioning Ion to discover exactly what they are[8]. He would be convinced by reason rather than stirred by an appeal to feeling. Accordingly he more than once politely evades Ion's attempt to indulge in quotation, and when at length the rhapsode, not to be denied, avails himself of the opportunity offered of declaiming a passage, he brings the performance to a close.

So too Ion's ignorance serves to throw into relief Socrates'

---

[1] 542 A.　　　　[2] 536 D.　　　　[3] 531 D: 540 A.
[4] 533 C: 536 D.　　[5] 539 E: cf. 536 E.　[6] 540 D: 541 C.
[7] 532 D.　　　　[8] 531 A.

superior powers of dialectic. The philosopher's persistency
in argument is more than a match for the rhapsode's
obstinacy.   Socrates indeed seems actually to find a
pleasure in throwing his opponent into confusion[1]. The
distinctions drawn by Ion are submitted to scrutiny and
proved invalid. His reiterations and denials are met un-
failingly by a further examination of the facts. Whereas
Ion appeals to feeling, Socrates relies upon the facts of
experience[2]. In short, he stands forth in the dialogue as a
type of matured and reflecting reason, seeking ever after
truth, and seasoned with a humanity and a humour, a little
cynical perhaps, but never morose or unkindly.

THE DRAMATIC DATE OF THE DIALOGUE.

The date at which the conversation between Socrates and
Ion is supposed to have taken place is not a point of great
importance nor is it possible accurately to determine it. The
mention in 541 D of the appointment of Phanosthenes the
Andrian to a command in the Athenian service, taken in
conjunction with the statement in Xenophon, *Hellenica*, I.
5. 18, that Phanosthenes was sent in 407–6 B.C. to succeed
Conon as general at Andros, might seem to suggest that the
dialogue took place later than that date.   But Phanosthenes
may have been employed as general on a former occasion or
Plato may have been guilty of an anachronistic reference
to his appointment in 407–6 B.C. On the whole, however,
although certainty is impossible, there seems to be no objec-
tion to placing the encounter between the philosopher and
the rhapsode about 405 B.C. during the concluding stage of
the Peloponnesian war.

[1] *e.g.* 540 E.   [2] 541 C, D.

THE MANUSCRIPTS.

The writings of Plato were arranged by Thrasyllus (1st cent. A.D.) in groups of four, styled tetralogies, the *Ion* being the third member of the seventh tetralogy. These tetralogies appear subsequently to have been distributed between two volumes, the first volume including tetralogies I—VII. The two leading manuscripts of Plato, the one in the Bodleian Library at Oxford (Cod. Bodleianus, MS. E. D. Clarke 39) and the other at Paris (Cod. Parisinus 1807), have each suffered the loss of one volume, the Paris manuscript presenting only the second of the two, and the Bodleian the first. In addition the Bodleian manuscript has been deprived of the last, the seventh, tetralogy of the first volume.

For the text of the *Ion* therefore we have to seek the aid of other manuscripts. The most important of these is in the Library of St Mark at Venice (Cod. Venetus Append. Class. 4 cod. 1) and is denoted by the letter T. This manuscript, which belongs perhaps to the tenth century, was copied from a good original ; there are very few omissions and practically nowhere is the text presented wholly unintelligible. In several places this MS. alone appears to preserve the genuine reading. Indications of change in the order of words are inserted by the writer, as well as corrections and variant readings in the margin. The scribe appears to have been a man of some education.

There are also two Vienna manuscripts, Cod. Vindobonensis 54 supp. phil. Gr. 7 denoted by the letter W and Cod. Vindobonensis 55 supp. phil. Gr. 39 denoted by the letter F. The first of these W which was brought to Vienna from Florence approximates in some places to the Bodleian MS., but in others to the Venetian T. In other places again it preserves a reading apparently old but differing from those of both the Bodleian and the Venetian. It contains in the margin a very large number of variant readings. The second MS. F is derived from a source differing from those of both T and W. It has suffered from interpolations at the hands of a Byzantine scholar, but it is noteworthy that the quotations from Homer in the *Ion* have not been corrected to agree with the text of the poet.

In addition there is a second Venetian manuscript, Cod. Venetus Marcianus 189 denoted by the letter S. So far as the text of the *Ion* is concerned this manuscript seems to be derived from the same source as the Vienna manuscript F.

Later writers such as the makers of anthologies like Stobaeus (date uncertain) occasionally quote passages from Plato. The evidence for the text afforded by such quotations, made possibly from memory, cannot be regarded as very weighty, but it is interesting and may at times prove of service in supporting the reading of one MS. against another.

The present edition follows in the main the tradition of the Codex Venetus (T). Variations from the readings of that MS. will be found indicated in the notes at the foot of the text.

ΙΩΝ

ΤΑ ΤΟΥ ΔΙΑΛΟΓΟΥ ΠΡΟΣΩΠΑ
ΣΩΚΡΑΤΗΣ, ΙΩΝ.

Ι. Τὸν Ἴωνα χαίρειν. πόθεν τὰ νῦν ἡμῖν ἐπιδεδήμηκας; ἢ οἴκοθεν ἐξ Ἐφέσου;

ΙΩΝ. Οὐδαμῶς, ὦ Σώκρατες, ἀλλ᾽ ἐξ Ἐπιδαύρου ἐκ τῶν Ἀσκληπιείων.

ΣΩ. Μῶν καὶ ῥαψῳδῶν ἀγῶνα τιθέασι τῷ θεῷ 5 οἱ Ἐπιδαύριοι;

ΙΩΝ. Πάνυ γε, καὶ τῆς ἄλλης γε μουσικῆς.

ΣΩ. Τί οὖν; ἠγωνίζου τι ἡμῖν; καὶ πῶς τι ἠγωνίσω;

ΙΩΝ. Τὰ πρῶτα τῶν ἄθλων ἠνεγκάμεθα, ὦ Σώ- 10 κρατες.

B   ΣΩ. Εὖ λέγεις· ἄγε δὴ ὅπως καὶ τὰ Παναθήναια νικήσομεν.

ΙΩΝ. Ἀλλ᾽ ἔσται ταῦτα, ἐὰν θεὸς ἐθέλῃ.

ΣΩ. Καὶ μὴν πολλάκις γε ἐζήλωσα ὑμᾶς τοὺς 15 ῥαψῳδούς, ὦ Ἴων, τῆς τέχνης· τὸ γὰρ ἅμα μὲν τὸ σῶμα κεκοσμῆσθαι ἀεὶ πρέπον ὑμῶν εἶναι τῇ τέχνῃ καὶ ὡς καλλίστοις φαίνεσθαι, ἅμα δὲ ἀναγκαῖον εἶναι ἔν τε ἄλλοις ποιηταῖς διατρίβειν πολλοῖς καὶ ἀγαθοῖς καὶ δὴ καὶ μάλιστα ἐν Ὁμήρῳ, τῷ ἀρίστῳ καὶ 20 θειοτάτῳ τῶν ποιητῶν, καὶ τὴν τούτου διάνοιαν

M.   I

2 ΠΛΑΤΩΝΟΣ

ἐκμανθάνειν, μὴ μόνον τὰ ἔπη, ζηλωτόν ἐστιν. οὐ γὰρ C
ἂν γένοιτό ποτε ῥαψῳδός, εἰ μὴ συνείη τὰ λεγόμενα
ὑπὸ τοῦ ποιητοῦ. τὸν γὰρ ῥαψῳδὸν ἑρμηνέα δεῖ τοῦ
ποιητοῦ τῆς διανοίας γίγνεσθαι τοῖς ἀκούουσι· τοῦτο
5 δὲ καλῶς ποιεῖν μὴ γιγνώσκοντα ὅ τι λέγει ὁ ποιητὴς
ἀδύνατον. ταῦτα οὖν πάντα ἄξια ζηλοῦσθαι.

ΙΙ. ΙΩΝ. Ἀληθῆ λέγεις, ὦ Σώκρατες· ἐμοὶ
γοῦν τοῦτο πλεῖστον ἔργον παρέσχε τῆς τέχνης, καὶ
οἶμαι κάλλιστα ἀνθρώπων λέγειν περὶ Ὁμήρου, ὡς
10 οὔτε Μητρόδωρος ὁ Λαμψακηνὸς οὔτε Στησίμβροτος D
ὁ Θάσιος οὔτε Γλαύκων οὔτε ἄλλος οὐδεὶς τῶν πώποτε
γενομένων ἔσχεν εἰπεῖν οὕτω πολλὰς καὶ καλὰς
διανοίας περὶ Ὁμήρου, ὅσας ἐγώ.

ΣΩ. Εὖ λέγεις, ὦ Ἴων· δῆλον γὰρ ὅτι οὐ
15 φθονήσεις μοι ἐπιδεῖξαι.

ΙΩΝ. Καὶ μὴν ἄξιόν γε ἀκοῦσαι, ὦ Σώκρατες,
ὡς εὖ κεκόσμηκα τὸν Ὅμηρον· ὥστε οἶμαι ὑπὸ
Ὁμηριδῶν ἄξιος εἶναι χρυσῷ στεφάνῳ στεφανωθῆναι.

ΣΩ. Καὶ μὴν ἐγὼ ἔτι ποιήσομαι σχολὴν ἀκροᾶ-
20 σθαί σου· νῦν δέ μοι τοσόνδε ἀπόκριναι· πότερον 531
περὶ Ὁμήρου μόνον δεινὸς εἶ ἢ καὶ περὶ Ἡσιόδου καὶ
Ἀρχιλόχου;

ΙΩΝ. Οὐδαμῶς, ἀλλὰ περὶ Ὁμήρου μόνον·
ἱκανὸν γάρ μοι δοκεῖ εἶναι.

25 ΣΩ. Ἔστι δὲ περὶ ὅτου Ὅμηρός τε καὶ Ἡσίοδος
ταὐτὰ λέγετον;

ΙΩΝ. Οἶμαι ἔγωγε καὶ πολλά.

2 συνείη F: συνίη T: συνιείη W   7-8 ἐμοὶ γοῦν WF:
ἐμοί γ' οὖν T   16 γε F: om. TW

ΣΩ. Πότερον οὖν περὶ τούτων κάλλιον ἂν
ἐξηγήσαιο ἃ Ὅμηρος λέγει ἢ ἃ Ἡσίοδος;

ΙΩΝ. Ὁμοίως ἂν περί γε τούτων, ὦ Σώκρατες,
περὶ ὧν ταὐτὰ λέγουσιν.

B ΣΩ. Τί δέ; ὧν πέρι μὴ ταὐτὰ λέγουσιν; οἷον περὶ 5
μαντικῆς λέγει τι Ὅμηρός τε καὶ Ἡσίοδος;

ΙΩΝ. Πάνυ γε.

ΣΩ. Τί οὖν; ὅσα τε ὁμοίως καὶ ὅσα διαφόρως
περὶ μαντικῆς λέγετον τὼ ποιητὰ τούτω, πότερον σὺ
κάλλιον ἂν ἐξηγήσαιο ἢ τῶν μάντεών τις τῶν 10
ἀγαθῶν;

ΙΩΝ. Τῶν μάντεων.

ΣΩ. Εἰ δὲ σὺ ἦσθα μάντις, οὐκ, εἴπερ περὶ τῶν
ὁμοίως λεγομένων οἷός τ᾽ ἦσθα ἐξηγήσασθαι, καὶ περὶ
τῶν διαφόρως λεγομένων ἠπίστω ἂν ἐξηγεῖσθαι; 15

ΙΩΝ. Δῆλον ὅτι.

C ΣΩ. Τί οὖν ποτὲ περὶ μὲν Ὁμήρου δεινὸς εἶ,
περὶ δὲ Ἡσιόδου οὔ, οὐδὲ τῶν ἄλλων ποιητῶν; ἢ
Ὅμηρος περὶ ἄλλων τινῶν λέγει ἢ ὦνπερ σύμπαντες
οἱ ἄλλοι ποιηταί; οὐ περὶ πολέμου τε τὰ πολλὰ 20
διελήλυθε καὶ περὶ ὁμιλιῶν πρὸς ἀλλήλους ἀνθρώπων
ἀγαθῶν τε καὶ κακῶν καὶ ἰδιωτῶν καὶ δημιουργῶν,
καὶ περὶ θεῶν πρὸς ἀλλήλους καὶ πρὸς ἀνθρώπους
ὁμιλούντων, ὡς ὁμιλοῦσι, καὶ περὶ τῶν οὐρανίων
παθημάτων καὶ περὶ τῶν ἐν Ἅιδου, καὶ γενέσεις καὶ 25
D θεῶν καὶ ἡρώων; οὐ ταῦτά ἐστι περὶ ὧν Ὅμηρος τὴν
ποίησιν πεποίηκεν;

ΙΩΝ. Ἀληθῆ λέγεις, ὦ Σώκρατες.

III. ΣΩ. Τί δέ; οἱ ἄλλοι ποιηταὶ οὐ περὶ τῶν
αὐτῶν τούτων; 30

4　　　ΠΛΑΤΩΝΟΣ

ΙΩΝ. Ναί, ἀλλ', ὦ Σώκρατες, οὐχ ὁμοίως πε-
ποιήκασι καὶ Ὅμηρος.

ΣΩ. Τί μήν; κάκιον;

ΙΩΝ. Πολύ γε.

5　ΣΩ. Ὅμηρος δὲ ἄμεινον;

ΙΩΝ. Ἄμεινον μέντοι νὴ Δία.

ΣΩ. Οὐκοῦν, ὦ φίλη κεφαλὴ Ἴων, ὅταν περὶ
ἀριθμοῦ πολλῶν λεγόντων εἷς τις ἄριστα λέγῃ,
γνώσεται δήπου τις τὸν εὖ λέγοντα;

10　ΙΩΝ. Φημί.　　　　　　　　　　　　　　　　E

ΣΩ. Πότερον οὖν ὁ αὐτός, ὅσπερ καὶ τοὺς κακῶς
λέγοντας, ἢ ἄλλος;

ΙΩΝ. Ὁ αὐτὸς δήπου.

ΣΩ. Οὐκοῦν ὁ τὴν ἀριθμητικὴν τέχνην ἔχων
15　οὗτός ἐστιν;

ΙΩΝ. Ναί.

ΣΩ. Τί δ', ὅταν πολλῶν λεγόντων περὶ
ὑγιεινῶν σιτίων, ὁποῖά ἐστιν, εἷς τις ἄριστα λέγῃ,
πότερον ἕτερος μέν τις τὸν ἄριστα λέγοντα γνώ-
20　σεται ὅτι ἄριστα λέγει, ἕτερος δὲ τὸν κάκιον, ἢ ὁ
αὐτός;

ΙΩΝ. Δῆλον δήπου, ὁ αὐτός.

ΣΩ. Τίς οὗτος; τί ὄνομα αὐτῷ;

ΙΩΝ. Ἰατρός.

25　ΣΩ. Οὐκοῦν ἐν κεφαλαίῳ λέγομεν, ὡς ὁ αὐτὸς
γνώσεται ἀεί, περὶ τῶν αὐτῶν πολλῶν λεγόντων,
ὅστις τε εὖ λέγει καὶ ὅστις κακῶς· ἢ εἰ μὴ γνώσεται 532
τὸν κακῶς λέγοντα, δῆλον ὅτι οὐδὲ τὸν εὖ, περί γε
τοῦ αὐτοῦ.

20–21 ὁ αὐτός F : αὐτός TW　　25 λέγομεν W : λέγωμεν T

ΙΩΝ. Οὕτως.

ΣΩ. Οὐκοῦν ὁ αὐτὸς γίγνεται δεινὸς περὶ ἀμφοτέρων ;

ΙΩΝ. Ναί.

ΣΩ. Οὐκοῦν σὺ φῂς καὶ Ὅμηρον καὶ τοὺς ἄλλους 5
ποιητάς, ἐν οἷς καὶ Ἡσίοδος καὶ Ἀρχίλοχός ἐστι,
περί γε τῶν αὐτῶν λέγειν, ἀλλ᾽ οὐχ ὁμοίως, ἀλλὰ
τὸν μὲν εὖ γε, τοὺς δὲ χεῖρον ;

ΙΩΝ. Καὶ ἀληθῆ λέγω.

ΣΩ. Οὐκοῦν, εἴπερ τὸν εὖ λέγοντα γιγνώσκεις, 10
B καὶ τοὺς χεῖρον λέγοντας γιγνώσκοις ἂν ὅτι χεῖρον
λέγουσιν.

ΙΩΝ. Ἔοικέ γε.

ΣΩ. Οὐκοῦν, ὦ βέλτιστε, ὁμοίως τὸν Ἴωνα
λέγοντες περὶ Ὁμήρου τε δεινὸν εἶναι καὶ περὶ τῶν 15
ἄλλων ποιητῶν οὐχ ἁμαρτησόμεθα, ἐπειδή γε αὐτὸς
ὁμολογεῖ τὸν αὐτὸν ἔσεσθαι κριτὴν ἱκανὸν πάντων,
ὅσοι ἂν περὶ τῶν αὐτῶν λέγωσι, τοὺς δὲ ποιητὰς
σχεδὸν ἅπαντας τὰ αὐτὰ ποιεῖν.

IV. ΙΩΝ. Τί οὖν ποτὲ τὸ αἴτιον, ὦ Σώκρατες, 20
ὅτι ἐγώ, ὅταν μέν τις περὶ ἄλλου του ποιητοῦ δια-
C λέγηται, οὔτε προσέχω τὸν νοῦν ἀδυνατῶ τε καὶ
ὁτιοῦν συμβαλέσθαι λόγου ἄξιον, ἀλλ᾽ ἀτεχνῶς
νυστάζω, ἐπειδὰν δέ τις περὶ Ὁμήρου μνησθῇ, εὐθύς
τε ἐγρήγορα καὶ προσέχω τὸν νοῦν καὶ εὐπορῶ ὅ τι 25
λέγω ;

ΣΩ. Οὐ χαλεπὸν τοῦτό γε εἰκάσαι, ὦ ἑταῖρε,
ἀλλὰ παντὶ δῆλον ὅτι τέχνῃ καὶ ἐπιστήμῃ περὶ
Ὁμήρου λέγειν ἀδύνατος εἶ· εἰ γὰρ τέχνῃ οἷός τε
ἦσθα, καὶ περὶ τῶν ἄλλων ποιητῶν ἁπάντων λέγειν 30

οἷός τ' ἂν ἦσθα· ποιητικὴ γάρ πού ἐστι τὸ ὅλον.
ἢ οὔ;

ΙΩΝ. Ναί.

ΣΩ. Οὐκοῦν ἐπειδὰν λάβῃ τις καὶ ἄλλην τέχνην D
5 ἡντινοῦν ὅλην, ὁ αὐτὸς τρόπος τῆς σκέψεώς ἐστι περὶ
ἀπασῶν τῶν τεχνῶν; πῶς τοῦτο λέγω, δέει τί μου
ἀκοῦσαι, ὦ Ἴων;

ΙΩΝ. Ναὶ μὰ τὸν Δί', ὦ Σώκρατες, ἔγωγε· χαίρω
γὰρ ἀκούων ὑμῶν τῶν σοφῶν.

10 ΣΩ. Βουλοίμην ἄν σε ἀληθῆ λέγειν, ὦ Ἴων·
ἀλλὰ σοφοὶ μέν πού ἐστε ὑμεῖς οἱ ῥαψῳδοὶ καὶ
ὑποκριταὶ καὶ ὧν ὑμεῖς ᾄδετε τὰ ποιήματα, ἐγὼ δὲ
οὐδὲν ἄλλο ἢ τἀληθῆ λέγω, οἷον εἰκὸς ἰδιώτην ἄνθρωπον. ἐπεὶ καὶ περὶ τούτου οὗ νῦν ἠρόμην σε, E
15 θέασαι ὡς φαῦλον καὶ ἰδιωτικόν ἐστι καὶ παντὸς
ἀνδρὸς γνῶναι ὃ ἔλεγον, τὴν αὐτὴν εἶναι σκέψιν,
ἐπειδάν τις ὅλην τέχνην λάβῃ. λάβωμεν γὰρ τῷ
λόγῳ· γραφικὴ γάρ τίς ἐστι τέχνη τὸ ὅλον;

ΙΩΝ. Ναί.

20 ΣΩ. Οὐκοῦν καὶ γραφεῖς πολλοὶ καὶ εἰσὶ καὶ
γεγόνασιν ἀγαθοὶ καὶ φαῦλοι;

ΙΩΝ. Πάνυ γε.

ΣΩ. Ἤδη οὖν τινὰ εἶδες, ὅστις περὶ μὲν Πολυγνώτου τοῦ Ἀγλαοφῶντος δεινός ἐστιν ἀποφαίνειν, ἃ
25 εὖ τε γράφει καὶ ἃ μή, περὶ δὲ τῶν ἄλλων γραφέων
ἀδύνατος; καὶ ἐπειδὰν μέν τις τὰ τῶν ἄλλων ζω- 533
γράφων ἔργα ἐπιδεικνύῃ, νυστάζει τε καὶ ἀπορεῖ
καὶ οὐκ ἔχει ὅ τι συμβάληται, ἐπειδὰν δὲ περὶ

Πολυγνώτου ἢ ἄλλου ὅτου βούλει τῶν γραφέων ἑνὸς
μόνου δέῃ ἀποφήνασθαι γνώμην, ἐγρήγορέ τε καὶ
προσέχει τὸν νοῦν καὶ εὐπορεῖ ὅ τι εἴπῃ;
ΙΩΝ. Οὐ μὰ τὸν Δία, οὐ δῆτα.

ΣΩ. Τί δέ; ἐν ἀνδριαντοποιίᾳ ἤδη τιν' εἶδες, 5
ὅστις περὶ μὲν Δαιδάλου τοῦ Μητίονος ἢ Ἐπειοῦ τοῦ
Β Πανοπέως ἢ Θεοδώρου τοῦ Σαμίου ἢ ἄλλου τινὸς
ἀνδριαντοποιοῦ ἑνὸς πέρι δεινός ἐστιν ἐξηγεῖσθαι ἃ
εὖ πεποίηκεν, ἐν δὲ τοῖς τῶν ἄλλων ἀνδριαντοποιῶν
ἔργοις ἀπορεῖ τε καὶ νυστάζει, οὐκ ἔχων ὅ τι εἴπῃ;   10
ΙΩΝ. Οὐ μὰ τὸν Δία, οὐδὲ τοῦτον ἑώρακα.

ΣΩ. Ἀλλὰ μήν, ὥς γ' ἐγὼ οἶμαι, οὐδ' ἐν αὐλήσει
γε οὐδὲ ἐν κιθαρίσει οὐδὲ ἐν κιθαρῳδίᾳ οὐδὲ ἐν
ῥαψῳδίᾳ οὐδεπώποτ' εἶδες ἄνδρα, ὅστις περὶ μὲν
Ϲ Ὀλύμπου δεινός ἐστιν ἐξηγεῖσθαι ἢ περὶ Θαμύρου ἢ 15
περὶ Ὀρφέως ἢ περὶ Φημίου τοῦ Ἰθακησίου ῥαψῳδοῦ,
περὶ δὲ Ἴωνος τοῦ Ἐφεσίου ἀπορεῖ καὶ οὐκ ἔχει
συμβαλέσθαι, ἅ τε εὖ ῥαψῳδεῖ καὶ ἃ μή.

ΙΩΝ. Οὐκ ἔχω σοι περὶ τούτου ἀντιλέγειν, ὦ
Σώκρατες· ἀλλ' ἐκεῖνο ἐμαυτῷ σύνοιδα, ὅτι περὶ 20
Ὁμήρου κάλλιστ' ἀνθρώπων λέγω καὶ εὐπορῶ καὶ οἱ
ἄλλοι πάντες μέ φασιν εὖ λέγειν, περὶ δὲ τῶν ἄλλων
οὔ. καίτοι ὅρα τοῦτο τί ἔστιν.

V. ΣΩ. Καὶ ὁρῶ, ὦ Ἴων, καὶ ἔρχομαι γέ σοι
D ἀποφαινόμενος, ὅ μοι δοκεῖ τοῦτο εἶναι. ἔστι γὰρ 25
τοῦτο τέχνη μὲν <οὔ>, οὐκ ὂν παρὰ σοὶ περὶ Ὁμήρου
εὖ λέγειν, ὃ νῦν δὴ ἔλεγον, θεία δὲ δύναμις, ἥ σε κινεῖ,
ὥσπερ ἐν τῇ λίθῳ, ἣν Εὐριπίδης μὲν Μαγνῆτιν

18 συμβάλλεσθαι Τ   24 ἔρχομαι F: ἄρχομαι TW   26 τέχνη
WF Stobaeus: τέχνῃ Τ | οὔ om. MSS.

ὠνόμασεν, οἱ δὲ πολλοὶ Ἡρακλείαν. καὶ γὰρ αὕτη
ἡ λίθος οὐ μόνον αὐτοὺς τοὺς δακτυλίους ἄγει τοὺς
σιδηροῦς, ἀλλὰ καὶ δύναμιν ἐντίθησι τοῖς δακτυλίοις,
ὥστε δύνασθαι ταὐτὸν τοῦτο ποιεῖν ὅπερ ἡ λίθος,
5 ἄλλους ἄγειν δακτυλίους, ὥστ' ἐνίοτε ὁρμαθὸς μακρὸς Ε
πάνυ σιδηρίων [καὶ δακτυλίων] ἐξ ἀλλήλων ἤρτηται·
πᾶσι δὲ τούτοις ἐξ ἐκείνης τῆς λίθου ἡ δύναμις
ἀνήρτηται. οὕτω δὲ καὶ ἡ Μοῦσα ἐνθέους μὲν ποιεῖ
αὐτή, διὰ δὲ τῶν ἐνθέων τούτων ἄλλων ἐνθουσιαζόντων
10 ὁρμαθὸς ἐξαρτᾶται. πάντες γὰρ οἵ τε τῶν ἐπῶν
ποιηταὶ οἱ ἀγαθοὶ οὐκ ἐκ τέχνης ἀλλ' ἔνθεοι ὄντες
καὶ κατεχόμενοι πάντα ταῦτα τὰ καλὰ λέγουσι
ποιήματα, καὶ οἱ μελοποιοὶ οἱ ἀγαθοὶ ὡσαύτως, ὥσπερ 534
οἱ κορυβαντιῶντες οὐκ ἔμφρονες ὄντες ὀρχοῦνται,
15 οὕτω καὶ οἱ μελοποιοὶ οὐκ ἔμφρονες ὄντες τὰ καλὰ
μέλη ταῦτα ποιοῦσιν, ἀλλ' ἐπειδὰν ἐμβῶσιν εἰς τὴν
ἁρμονίαν καὶ εἰς τὸν ῥυθμόν, βακχεύουσι καὶ κατεχόμενοι, ὥσπερ αἱ βάκχαι ἀρύτονται ἐκ τῶν ποταμῶν
μέλι καὶ γάλα κατεχόμεναι, ἔμφρονες δὲ οὖσαι οὔ,
20 καὶ τῶν μελοποιῶν ἡ ψυχὴ τοῦτο ἐργάζεται, ὅπερ
αὐτοὶ λέγουσι. λέγουσι γὰρ δήπουθεν πρὸς ἡμᾶς οἱ
ποιηταί, ὅτι ἀπὸ κρηνῶν μελιρρύτων ἐκ Μουσῶν Β
κήπων τινῶν καὶ ναπῶν δρεπόμενοι τὰ μέλη ἡμῖν
φέρουσιν ὥσπερ αἱ μέλιτται, καὶ αὐτοὶ οὕτω πετ-
25 όμενοι· καὶ ἀληθῆ λέγουσι· κοῦφον γὰρ χρῆμα
ποιητής ἐστι καὶ πτηνὸν καὶ ἱερόν, καὶ οὐ πρότερον
οἷός τε ποιεῖν, πρὶν ἂν ἔνθεός τε γένηται καὶ ἔκφρων

2 ἄγει om. T   6 καὶ δακτυλίων del. Hermann   9 αὐτή F
Stobaeus: αὕτη TW   17 βακχεύουσι F Stobaeus: καὶ βακχεύουσι
TW   18 ἀρύονται WF Stobaeus: But cf. Phaedrus 253 A

καὶ ὁ νοῦς μηκέτι ἐν αὐτῷ ἐνῇ· ἕως δ' ἂν τουτὶ ἔχῃ
τὸ κτῆμα, ἀδύνατος πᾶς ποιεῖν ἄνθρωπός ἐστιν καὶ
χρησμῳδεῖν. ἄτε οὖν οὐ τέχνῃ ποιοῦντες καὶ πολλὰ
λέγοντες καὶ καλὰ περὶ τῶν πραγμάτων, ὥσπερ σὺ
C περὶ Ὁμήρου, ἀλλὰ θείᾳ μοίρᾳ, τοῦτο μόνον οἷός τε 5
ἕκαστος ποιεῖν καλῶς, ἐφ' ὃ ἡ Μοῦσα αὐτὸν ὥρμησεν,
ὁ μὲν διθυράμβους, ὁ δὲ ἐγκώμια, ὁ δὲ ὑπορχήματα,
ὁ δ' ἔπη, ὁ δ' ἰάμβους· τὰ δ' ἄλλα φαῦλος αὐτῶν
ἕκαστός ἐστιν. οὐ γὰρ τέχνῃ ταῦτα λέγουσιν, ἀλλὰ
θείᾳ δυνάμει, ἐπεί, εἰ περὶ ἑνὸς τέχνῃ καλῶς ἠπίσταντο 10
λέγειν, κἂν περὶ τῶν ἄλλων ἁπάντων· διὰ ταῦτα δὲ
ὁ θεὸς ἐξαιρούμενος τούτων τὸν νοῦν τούτοις χρῆται
ὑπηρέταις καὶ τοῖς χρησμῳδοῖς καὶ τοῖς μάντεσι τοῖς
D θείοις, ἵνα ἡμεῖς οἱ ἀκούοντες εἰδῶμεν, ὅτι οὐχ οὗτοί
εἰσιν οἱ ταῦτα λέγοντες οὕτω πολλοῦ ἄξια, οἷς νοῦς 15
μὴ πάρεστιν, ἀλλ' ὁ θεὸς αὐτός ἐστιν ὁ λέγων, διὰ
τούτων δὲ φθέγγεται πρὸς ἡμᾶς. μέγιστον δὲ τεκμήριον τῷ λόγῳ Τύννιχος ὁ Χαλκιδεύς, ὃς ἄλλο μὲν
οὐδὲν πώποτ' ἐποίησε ποίημα, ὅτου τις ἂν ἀξιώσειε
μνησθῆναι, τὸν δὲ παίωνα ὃν πάντες ᾄδουσι, σχεδόν 20
τι πάντων μελῶν κάλλιστον, ἀτεχνῶς, ὅπερ αὐτὸς
λέγει, εὕρημά τι Μοισᾶν. ἐν τούτῳ γὰρ δὴ μάλιστά
E μοι δοκεῖ ὁ θεὸς ἐνδείξασθαι ἡμῖν, ἵνα μὴ διστάζωμεν,
ὅτι οὐκ ἀνθρώπινά ἐστι τὰ καλὰ ταῦτα ποιήματα
οὐδὲ ἀνθρώπων, ἀλλὰ θεῖα καὶ θεῶν, οἱ δὲ ποιηταὶ 25
οὐδὲν ἀλλ' ἢ ἑρμηνεῖς εἰσὶ τῶν θεῶν, κατεχόμενοι ἐξ
ὅτου ἂν ἕκαστος κατέχηται. ταῦτα ἐνδεικνύμενος ὁ
θεὸς ἐξεπίτηδες διὰ τοῦ φαυλοτάτου ποιητοῦ τὸ

---

6 καλῶς WF: καλός T   22 εὕρημά τι Stephanus: εὑρήματι
TWF

κάλλιστον μέλος ἦσεν· ἢ οὐ δοκῶ σοι ἀληθῆ λέγειν, 535
ὦ Ἴων;

ΙΩΝ. Ναὶ μὰ τὸν Δία ἔμοιγε· ἅπτει γάρ πώς
μου τοῖς λόγοις τῆς ψυχῆς, ὦ Σώκρατες, καί μοι
5 δοκοῦσι θείᾳ μοίρᾳ ἡμῖν παρὰ τῶν θεῶν ταῦτα οἱ
ἀγαθοὶ ποιηταὶ ἑρμηνεύειν.

VI. ΣΩ. Οὐκοῦν ὑμεῖς αὖ οἱ ῥαψῳδοὶ τὰ τῶν
ποιητῶν ἑρμηνεύετε;

ΙΩΝ. Καὶ τοῦτο ἀληθὲς λέγεις.

10 ΣΩ. Οὐκοῦν ἑρμηνέων ἑρμηνεῖς γίγνεσθε;

ΙΩΝ. Παντάπασί γε.

ΣΩ. Ἔχε δή μοι τόδε εἰπέ, ὦ Ἴων, καὶ μὴ ἀπο- B
κρύψῃ ὅ τι ἄν σε ἔρωμαι· ὅταν εὖ εἴπῃς ἔπη καὶ
ἐκπλήξῃς μάλιστα τοὺς θεωμένους, ἢ τὸν Ὀδυσσέα
15 ὅταν ἐπὶ τὸν οὐδὸν ἐφαλλόμενον ᾄδῃς, ἐκφανῆ γιγνό-
μενον τοῖς μνηστῆρσι καὶ ἐκχέοντα τοὺς οἰστοὺς πρὸ
τῶν ποδῶν, ἢ Ἀχιλλέα ἐπὶ τὸν Ἕκτορα ὁρμῶντα, ἢ
καὶ τῶν περὶ Ἀνδρομάχην ἐλεινῶν τι ἢ περὶ Ἑκάβην
ἢ περὶ Πρίαμον, τότε πότερον ἔμφρων εἶ, ἢ ἔξω
20 σαυτοῦ γίγνει καὶ παρὰ τοῖς πράγμασιν οἴεταί C
σου εἶναι ἡ ψυχὴ οἷς λέγεις ἐνθουσιάζουσα, ἢ
ἐν Ἰθάκῃ οὖσιν ἢ ἐν Τροίᾳ ἢ ὅπως ἂν καὶ τὰ
ἔπη ἔχῃ;

ΙΩΝ. Ὡς ἐναργές μοι τοῦτο, ὦ Σώκρατες, τὸ
25 τεκμήριον εἶπες· οὐ γάρ σε ἀποκρυψάμενος ἐρῶ.
ἐγὼ γὰρ ὅταν ἐλεινόν τι λέγω, δακρύων ἐμπίπλανταί
μου οἱ ὀφθαλμοί· ὅταν τε φοβερὸν ἢ δεινόν, ὀρθαὶ
αἱ τρίχες ἵστανται ὑπὸ φόβου καὶ ἡ καρδία
πηδᾷ.

D ΣΩ. Τί οὖν; φῶμεν, ὦ Ἴων, ἔμφρονα εἶναι τότε τοῦτον τὸν ἄνθρωπον, ὃς ἂν κεκοσμημένος ἐσθῆτι ποικίλῃ καὶ χρυσοῖς στεφάνοις κλάῃ τ᾽ ἐν θυσίαις καὶ ἑορταῖς, μηδὲν ἀπολωλεκὼς τούτων, ἢ φοβῆται πλέον ἢ ἐν δισμυρίοις ἀνθρώποις ἑστηκὼς φιλίοις, 5 μηδενὸς ἀποδύοντος μηδὲ ἀδικοῦντος;

ΙΩΝ. Οὐ μὰ τὸν Δία, οὐ πάνυ, ὦ Σώκρατες, ὥς γε τἀληθὲς εἰρῆσθαι.

ΣΩ. Οἶσθα οὖν ὅτι καὶ τῶν θεατῶν τοὺς πολλοὺς ταὐτὰ ταῦτα ὑμεῖς ἐργάζεσθε; 10

E ΙΩΝ. Καὶ μάλα καλῶς οἶδα· καθορῶ γὰρ ἑκάστοτε αὐτοὺς ἄνωθεν ἀπὸ τοῦ βήματος κλάοντάς τε καὶ δεινὸν ἐμβλέποντας καὶ συνθαμβοῦντας τοῖς λεγομένοις. δεῖ γάρ με καὶ σφόδρ᾽ αὐτοῖς τὸν νοῦν προσέχειν· ὡς ἐὰν μὲν κλάοντας αὐτοὺς καθίσω, 15 αὐτὸς γελάσομαι ἀργύριον λαμβάνων, ἐὰν δὲ γελῶντας, αὐτὸς κλαύσομαι ἀργύριον ἀπολλύς.

VII. ΣΩ. Οἶσθα οὖν ὅτι οὗτός ἐστιν ὁ θεατὴς τῶν δακτυλίων ὁ ἔσχατος, ὧν ἐγὼ ἔλεγον ὑπὸ τῆς Ἡρακλειώτιδος λίθου ἀπ᾽ ἀλλήλων τὴν δύναμιν 20 λαμβάνειν; ὁ δὲ μέσος σὺ ὁ ῥαψῳδὸς καὶ ὑποκριτής, 536 ὁ δὲ πρῶτος αὐτὸς ὁ ποιητής· ὁ δὲ θεὸς διὰ πάντων τούτων ἕλκει τὴν ψυχὴν ὅποι ἂν βούληται τῶν ἀνθρώπων, ἀνακρεμαννὺς ἐξ ἀλλήλων τὴν δύναμιν. καὶ ὥσπερ ἐκ τῆς λίθου ἐκείνης ὁρμαθὸς πάμπολυς 25 ἐξήρτηται χορευτῶν τε καὶ διδασκάλων καὶ ὑποδιδασκάλων, ἐκ πλαγίου ἐξηρτημένων τῶν τῆς Μούσης ἐκκρεμαμένων δακτυλίων. καὶ ὁ μὲν τῶν ποιητῶν ἐξ ἄλλης Μούσης, ὁ δὲ ἐξ ἄλλης ἐξήρτηται· ὀνομάζομεν

1-2 τότε τοῦτον WF τοῦτον τότε T

δὲ αὐτὸ κατέχεται, τὸ δέ ἐστι παραπλήσιον· ἔχεται B
γάρ· ἐκ δὲ τούτων τῶν πρώτων δακτυλίων. τῶν
ποιητῶν, ἄλλοι ἐξ ἄλλου αὖ ἠρτημένοι εἰσὶ καὶ
ἐνθουσιάζουσιν, οἱ μὲν ἐξ Ὀρφέως, οἱ δὲ ἐκ Μουσαίου·
5 οἱ δὲ πολλοὶ ἐξ Ὁμήρου κατέχονταί τε καὶ ἔχονται.
ὧν σύ, ὦ Ἴων, εἷς εἶ καὶ κατέχει ἐξ Ὁμήρου, καὶ
ἐπειδὰν μέν τις ἄλλου του ποιητοῦ ᾄδῃ, καθεύδεις τε
καὶ ἀπορεῖς ὅ τι λέγῃς, ἐπειδὰν δὲ τούτου τοῦ ποιητοῦ
φθέγξηταί τις μέλος, εὐθὺς ἐγρήγορας καὶ ὀρχεῖταί
10 σου ἡ ψυχὴ καὶ εὐπορεῖς ὅ τι λέγῃς· οὐ γὰρ τέχνῃ C
οὐδ᾽ ἐπιστήμῃ περὶ Ὁμήρου λέγεις ἃ λέγεις, ἀλλὰ
θείᾳ μοίρᾳ καὶ κατοκωχῇ· ὥσπερ οἱ κορυβαντιῶντες
ἐκείνου μόνου αἰσθάνονται τοῦ μέλους ὀξέως, ὃ ἂν ᾖ
τοῦ θεοῦ ἐξ ὅτου ἂν κατέχωνται, καὶ εἰς ἐκεῖνο τὸ
15 μέλος καὶ σχημάτων καὶ ῥημάτων εὐποροῦσι, τῶν δὲ
ἄλλων οὐ φροντίζουσιν, οὕτω καὶ σύ, ὦ Ἴων, περὶ
μὲν Ὁμήρου ὅταν τις μνησθῇ, εὐπορεῖς, περὶ δὲ τῶν
ἄλλων ἀπορεῖς· τούτου δ᾽ ἐστὶ τὸ αἴτιον, ὅ μ᾽ ἐρωτᾷς, D
δι᾽ ὅ τι σὺ περὶ μὲν Ὁμήρου εὐπορεῖς, περὶ δὲ τῶν
20 ἄλλων οὔ, ὅτι οὐ τέχνῃ ἀλλὰ θείᾳ μοίρᾳ Ὁμήρου
δεινὸς εἶ ἐπαινέτης.

VIII. ΙΩΝ. Σὺ μὲν εὖ λέγεις, ὦ Σώκρατες·
θαυμάζοιμι μέντ᾽ ἂν εἰ οὕτως εὖ εἴποις, ὥστε με
ἀναπεῖσαι, ὡς ἐγὼ κατεχόμενος καὶ μαινόμενος
25 Ὅμηρον ἐπαινῶ. οἶμαι δὲ οὐδ᾽ ἂν σοὶ δόξαιμι,
εἴ μου ἀκούσαις λέγοντος περὶ Ὁμήρου.

ΣΩ. Καὶ μὴν ἐθέλω γε ἀκοῦσαι, οὐ μέντοι
πρότερον πρὶν ἄν μοι ἀποκρίνῃ τόδε· ὧν Ὅμηρος E

23 εἰ οὕτως F: οὕτως εἰ TW

λέγει περὶ τίνος εὖ λέγεις; οὐ γὰρ δήπου περὶ ἁπάντων γε.

ΙΩΝ. Εὖ ἴσθι, ὦ Σώκρατες, περὶ οὐδενὸς ὅτου οὔ.

ΣΩ. Οὐ δήπου καὶ περὶ τούτων, ὧν σὺ μὲν
τυγχάνεις οὐκ εἰδώς, Ὅμηρος δὲ λέγει.   5

ΙΩΝ. Καὶ ταῦτα ποῖά ἐστιν, ἃ Ὅμηρος μὲν
λέγει, ἐγὼ δὲ οὐκ οἶδα;

537   ΣΩ. Οὐ καὶ περὶ τεχνῶν μέντοι λέγει πολλαχοῦ
Ὅμηρος καὶ πολλά; οἷον καὶ περὶ ἡνιοχείας—ἐὰν
μνησθῶ τὰ ἔπη, ἐγώ σοι φράσω.   10

ΙΩΝ. Ἀλλ᾽ ἐγὼ ἐρῶ· ἐγὼ γὰρ μέμνημαι.

ΣΩ. Εἰπὲ δή μοι ἃ λέγει Νέστωρ Ἀντιλόχῳ τῷ
υἱεῖ, παραινῶν εὐλαβηθῆναι περὶ τὴν καμπὴν ἐν τῇ
ἱπποδρομίᾳ τῇ ἐπὶ Πατρόκλῳ.

ΙΩΝ.

Κλινθῆναι δέ, φησί, καὶ αὐτὸς ἐυξέστῳ ἐνὶ δίφρῳ   15
ἧκ᾽ ἐπ᾽ ἀριστερὰ τοῖιν· ἀτὰρ τὸν δεξιὸν ἵππον
B   κένσαι ὁμοκλήσας, εἶξαί τέ οἱ ἡνία χερσίν.
ἐν νύσσῃ δέ τοι ἵππος ἀριστερὸς ἐγχριμφθήτω,
ὡς ἄν τοι πλήμνη γε δοάσσεται ἄκρον ἱκέσθαι
κύκλου ποιητοῖο· λίθου δ᾽ ἀλέασθαι ἐπαυρεῖν.   20

ΣΩ. Ἀρκεῖ. ταῦτα δή, ὦ Ἴων, τὰ ἔπη εἴτε
C ὀρθῶς λέγει Ὅμηρος εἴτε μή, πότερος ἂν γνοίη ἄμεινον,
ἰατρὸς ἢ ἡνίοχος.

ΙΩΝ. Ἡνίοχος δήπου.

ΣΩ. Πότερον ὅτι τέχνην ταύτην ἔχει ἢ κατ᾽ ἄλλο 25
τι;

ΙΩΝ. Οὔκ, ἀλλ᾽ ὅτι τέχνην.

ΣΩ. Οὐκοῦν ἑκάστῃ τῶν τεχνῶν ἀποδέδοταί τι

1 λέγεις Cornarius: λέγει TWF   19 ἄν F: μή TW

ὑπὸ τοῦ θεοῦ ἔργον οἷά τε εἶναι γιγνώσκειν; οὐ γάρ
που ἃ κυβερνητικῇ γιγνώσκομεν, γνωσόμεθα καὶ
ἰατρικῇ.

ΙΩΝ. Οὐ δῆτα.

5 ΣΩ. Οὐδέ γε ἃ ἰατρικῇ, ταῦτα καὶ τεκτονικῇ.

ΙΩΝ. Οὐ δῆτα.

ΣΩ. Οὐκοῦν οὕτω καὶ κατὰ πασῶν τῶν τεχνῶν, D
ἃ τῇ ἑτέρᾳ τέχνῃ γιγνώσκομεν, οὐ γνωσόμεθα τῇ
ἑτέρᾳ; τόδε δέ μοι πρότερον τούτου ἀπόκριναι· τὴν
10 μὲν ἑτέραν φῂς εἶναί τινα τέχνην, τὴν δ᾽ ἑτέραν;

ΙΩΝ. Ναί.

ΣΩ. Ἆρα ὥσπερ ἐγὼ τεκμαιρόμενος, ὅταν ἡ μὲν
ἑτέρων πραγμάτων ᾖ ἐπιστήμη, ἡ δ᾽ ἑτέρων, οὕτω
καλῶ τὴν μὲν ἄλλην, τὴν δὲ ἄλλην τέχνην, οὕτω καὶ
15 σύ;

ΙΩΝ. Ναί.   E

ΣΩ. Εἰ γάρ που τῶν αὐτῶν πραγμάτων ἐπιστήμη εἴη τις, τί ἂν τὴν μὲν ἑτέραν φαῖμεν εἶναι, τὴν
δ᾽ ἑτέραν, ὁπότε γε ταὐτὰ εἴη εἰδέναι ἀπ᾽ ἀμφοτέρων,
20 ὥσπερ ἐγώ τε γιγνώσκω ὅτι πέντε εἰσὶν οὗτοι οἱ
δάκτυλοι, καὶ σύ, ὥσπερ ἐγώ, περὶ τούτων ταὐτὰ
γιγνώσκεις· καὶ εἴ σε ἐγὼ ἐροίμην, εἰ τῇ αὐτῇ τέχνῃ
γιγνώσκομεν τῇ ἀριθμητικῇ τὰ αὐτὰ ἐγώ τε καὶ σύ,
ἢ ἄλλῃ, φαίης ἂν δήπου τῇ αὐτῇ.

25 ΙΩΝ. Ναί.

ΣΩ. Ὁ τοίνυν ἄρτι ἔμελλον ἐρήσεσθαί σε, νυνὶ 538
εἰπέ, εἰ κατὰ πασῶν τῶν τεχνῶν οὕτω σοι δοκεῖ, τῇ
μὲν αὐτῇ τέχνῃ τὰ αὐτὰ ἀναγκαῖον εἶναι γιγνώσκειν,
τῇ δ᾽ ἑτέρᾳ μὴ τὰ αὐτά, ἀλλ᾽ εἴπερ ἄλλη ἐστίν,
30 ἀναγκαῖον καὶ ἕτερα γιγνώσκειν.

ΙΩΝ. Οὕτω μοι δοκεῖ, ὦ Σώκρατες.

ΙΧ. ΣΩ. Οὐκοῦν ὅστις ἂν μὴ ἔχῃ τινὰ τέχνην, ταύτης τῆς τέχνης τὰ λεγόμενα ἢ πραττόμενα καλῶς γιγνώσκειν οὐχ οἷός τ᾽ ἔσται;

B ΙΩΝ. Ἀληθῆ λέγεις.   5

ΣΩ. Πότερον οὖν περὶ τῶν ἐπῶν ὧν εἶπες, εἴτε καλῶς λέγει Ὅμηρος εἴτε μή, σὺ κάλλιον γνώσει ἢ ἡνίοχος;

ΙΩΝ. Ἡνίοχος.

ΣΩ. Ῥαψῳδὸς γάρ που εἶ, ἀλλ᾽ οὐχ ἡνίοχος.   10

ΙΩΝ. Ναί.

ΣΩ. Ἡ δὲ ῥαψῳδικὴ τέχνη ἑτέρα ἐστὶ τῆς ἡνιοχικῆς;

ΙΩΝ. Ναί.

ΣΩ. Εἰ ἄρα ἑτέρα, περὶ ἑτέρων καὶ ἐπιστήμη 15 πραγμάτων ἐστίν.

ΙΩΝ. Ναί.

ΣΩ. Τί δὲ δή, ὅταν Ὅμηρος λέγῃ, ὡς τετρωμένῳ
C τῷ Μαχάονι Ἑκαμήδη ἡ Νέστορος παλλακὴ κυκεῶνα πίνειν δίδωσι; καὶ λέγει πως οὕτως·   20

οἴνῳ Πραμνείῳ, φησίν, ἐπὶ δ᾽ αἴγειον κνῆ τυρὸν
κνήστι χαλκείῃ· παρὰ δὲ κρόμυον ποτῷ ὄψον·

ταῦτα εἴτε ὀρθῶς λέγει Ὅμηρος εἴτε μή, πότερον ἰατρικῆς ἐστι διαγνῶναι καλῶς ἢ ῥαψῳδικῆς;

ΙΩΝ. Ἰατρικῆς.   25

ΣΩ. Τί δέ, ὅταν λέγῃ Ὅμηρος·
D   ἡ δὲ μολυβδαίνη ἰκέλη ἐς βυσσὸν ἵκανεν,

15–16 καὶ ἐπιστήμη πραγμάτων WF: πραγμάτων καὶ ἐπιστήμη T
22 κνήστι F: κνήστει TW

ἥ τε κατ' ἀγραύλοιο βοὸς κέρας ἐμμεμαυῖα
ἔρχεται ὠμηστῇσι μετ' ἰχθύσι πῆμα φέρουσα·
ταῦτα πότερον φῶμεν ἁλιευτικῆς εἶναι τέχνης μᾶλλον
κρῖναι ἢ ῥαψῳδικῆς, ἄττα λέγει καὶ εἴτε καλῶς εἴτε
5 μή;

ΙΩΝ. Δῆλον δή, ὦ Σώκρατες, ὅτι ἁλιευτικῆς.

ΣΩ. Σκέψαι δή, σοῦ ἐρομένου, εἰ ἔροιό με· ἐπειδὴ
τοίνυν, ὦ Σώκρατες, τούτων τῶν τεχνῶν ἐν Ὁμήρῳ Ε
εὑρίσκεις ἃ προσήκει ἑκάστῃ διακρίνειν, ἴθι μοι
10 ἔξευρε καὶ τὰ, τοῦ μάντεώς τε καὶ μαντικῆς, ποῖά
ἐστιν ἃ προσήκει αὐτῷ οἵῳ τ' εἶναι διαγιγνώσκειν,
εἴτε εὖ εἴτε κακῶς πεποίηται—σκέψαι ὡς ῥᾳδίως τε
καὶ ἀληθῆ ἐγώ σοι ἀποκρινοῦμαι. πολλαχοῦ μὲν
γὰρ καὶ ἐν Ὀδυσσείᾳ λέγει, οἷον καὶ ἃ ὁ τῶν
15 Μελαμποδιδῶν λέγει μάντις πρὸς τοὺς μνηστῆρας,
Θεοκλύμενος·

   δαιμόνιοι, τί κακὸν τόδε πάσχετε; νυκτὶ μὲν ὑμέων 539
   εἰλύαται κεφαλαί τε πρόσωπά τε νέρθε τε γυῖα,
   οἰμωγὴ δὲ δέδηε, δεδάκρυνται δὲ παρειαί·
20 εἰδώλων τε πλέον πρόθυρον, πλείη δὲ καὶ αὐλὴ
   ἱεμένων ἔρεβόσδε ὑπὸ ζόφον· ἠέλιος δὲ
   οὐρανοῦ ἐξαπόλωλε, κακὴ δ' ἐπιδέδρομεν ἀχλύς· Β
   πολλαχοῦ δὲ καὶ ἐν Ἰλιάδι, οἷον καὶ ἐπὶ τειχομαχίᾳ·
   λέγει γὰρ καὶ ἐνταῦθα·
25 ὄρνις γάρ σφιν ἐπῆλθε περησέμεναι μεμαῶσιν,
   αἰετὸς ὑψιπέτης, ἐπ' ἀριστερὰ λαὸν ἐέργων,
   φοινήεντα δράκοντα φέρων ὀνύχεσσι πέλωρον, C
   ζωόν, ἔτ' ἀσπαίροντα· καὶ οὔπω λήθετο χάρμης.

14 ἃ ante ὁ om. T   19 ὅέδῃε W : δέδῃαι T

κόψε γὰρ αὐτὸν ἔχοντα κατὰ στῆθος παρὰ δειρὴν
ἰδνωθεὶς ὀπίσω, ὁ δ᾽ ἀπὸ ἔθεν ἧκε χαμᾶζε
ἀλγήσας ὀδύνῃσι, μέσῳ δ᾽ ἐγκάββαλ᾽ ὁμίλῳ·
D αὐτὸς δὲ κλάγξας ἔπετο πνοιῆς ἀνέμοιο.
ταῦτα φήσω καὶ τὰ τοιαῦτα τῷ μάντει προσήκειν 5
καὶ σκοπεῖν καὶ κρίνειν.
  ΙΩΝ. Ἀληθῆ γε σὺ λέγων, ὦ Σώκρατες.
  Χ. ΣΩ. Καὶ σύ γε, ὦ Ἴων, ἀληθῆ ταῦτα λέγεις.
ἴθι δὴ καὶ σὺ ἐμοί, ὥσπερ ἐγὼ σοὶ ἐξέλεξα καὶ ἐξ
Ὀδυσσείας καὶ ἐξ Ἰλιάδος ὁποῖα τοῦ μάντεώς ἐστι 10
E καὶ ὁποῖα τοῦ ἰατροῦ καὶ ὁποῖα τοῦ ἁλιέως, οὕτω καὶ
σὺ ἐμοὶ ἔκλεξον, ἐπειδὴ καὶ ἐμπειρότερος εἶ ἐμοῦ τῶν
Ὁμήρου, ὁποῖα τοῦ ῥαψῳδοῦ ἐστίν, ὦ Ἴων, καὶ τῆς
ῥαψῳδικῆς, ἃ τῷ ῥαψῳδῷ προσήκει καὶ σκοπεῖσθαι
καὶ διακρίνειν παρὰ τοὺς ἄλλους ἀνθρώπους.   15
  ΙΩΝ. Ἐγὼ μέν φημι, ὦ Σώκρατες, ἅπαντα.
  ΣΩ. Οὐ σύ γε φῂς, ὦ Ἴων, ἅπαντα· ἢ οὕτως
ἐπιλήσμων εἶ; καίτοι οὐκ ἂν πρέποι γε ἐπιλήσμονα
εἶναι ῥαψῳδὸν ἄνδρα.
540 ΙΩΝ. Τί δὲ δὴ ἐπιλανθάνομαι;   20
  ΣΩ. Οὐ μέμνησαι ὅτι ἔφησθα τὴν ῥαψῳδικὴν
τέχνην ἑτέραν εἶναι τῆς ἡνιοχικῆς;
  ΙΩΝ. Μέμνημαι.
  ΣΩ. Οὐκοῦν καὶ ἑτέραν οὖσαν ἕτερα γνώσεσθαι
ὡμολόγεις;   25
  ΙΩΝ. Ναί.
  ΣΩ. Οὐκ ἄρα πάντα γε γνώσεται ἡ ῥαψῳδικὴ
κατὰ τὸν σὸν λόγον, οὐδὲ ὁ ῥαψῳδός.

2 ὀπίσω WF : ὀπίσσω T   3 ἐγκάββαλλ᾽, corr. ἐγκάββαλ᾽ T :
ἐνκάμβαλ᾽ W : ἐνὶ κάμβαλ᾽ F

ΙΩΝ. Πλήν γε ἴσως τὰ τοιαῦτα, ὦ Σώκρατες.

ΣΩ. Τὰ τοιαῦτα δὲ λέγεις πλὴν τὰ τῶν ἄλλων B τεχνῶν σχεδόν τι· ἀλλὰ ποῖα δὴ γνώσεται, ἐπειδὴ οὐχ ἅπαντα;

5 ΙΩΝ. ᾿Α πρέπει, οἶμαι ἔγωγε, ἀνδρὶ εἰπεῖν καὶ ὁποῖα γυναικί, καὶ ὁποῖα δούλῳ καὶ ὁποῖα ἐλευθέρῳ, καὶ ὁποῖα ἀρχομένῳ καὶ ὁποῖα ἄρχοντι.

ΣΩ. ᾿Αρ᾽ ὁποῖα ἄρχοντι, λέγεις, ἐν θαλάττῃ χειμαζομένου πλοίου πρέπει εἰπεῖν, ὁ ῥαψῳδὸς 10 γνώσεται κάλλιον ἢ ὁ κυβερνήτης;

ΙΩΝ. Οὔκ, ἀλλὰ ὁ κυβερνήτης τοῦτό γε.

ΣΩ. ᾿Αλλ᾽ ὁποῖα ἄρχοντι κάμνοντος πρέπει C εἰπεῖν, ὁ ῥαψῳδὸς γνώσεται κάλλιον ἢ ὁ ἰατρός;

ΙΩΝ. Οὐδὲ τοῦτο.

15 ΣΩ. ᾿Αλλ᾽ οἷα δούλῳ πρέπει, λέγεις;

ΙΩΝ. Ναί.

ΣΩ. Οἷον βουκόλῳ λέγεις δούλῳ ἃ πρέπει εἰπεῖν ἀγριαινουσῶν βοῶν παραμυθουμένῳ, ὁ ῥαψῳδὸς γνώσεται, ἀλλ᾽ οὐχ ὁ βουκόλος;

20 ΙΩΝ. Οὐ δῆτα.

ΣΩ. ᾿Αλλ᾽ οἷα γυναικὶ πρέποντά ἐστιν εἰπεῖν ταλασιουργῷ περὶ ἐρίων ἐργασίας; D

ΙΩΝ. Οὔ.

ΣΩ ᾿Αλλ᾽ οἷα ἀνδρὶ πρέπει εἰπεῖν γνώσεται 25 στρατηγῷ στρατιώταις παραινοῦντι;

ΙΩΝ. Ναί, τὰ τοιαῦτα γνώσεται ὁ ῥαψῳδός.

XI. ΣΩ. Τί δέ; ἡ ῥαψῳδικὴ τέχνη στρατηγικὴ ἐστιν;

11 ἀλλὰ ὁ W : ἀλλὰ καὶ ὁ T   12 κάμνοντος F : κάμνοντι TW
26 νή TWF

ΙΩΝ. Γνοίην γοῦν ἂν ἔγωγε οἷα στρατηγὸν πρέπει εἰπεῖν.

ΣΩ. Ἴσως γὰρ εἶ καὶ στρατηγικός, Ἴων. καὶ γὰρ εἰ ἐτύγχανες ἱππικὸς ὢν ἅμα καὶ κιθαριστικός, Ε ἔγνως ἂν ἵππους εὖ καὶ κακῶς ἱππαζομένους· ἀλλ' εἴ 5 σ' ἐγὼ ἠρόμην, ποτέρᾳ δὴ τέχνῃ, ὦ Ἴων, γιγνώσκεις τοὺς εὖ ἱππαζομένους ἵππους; ᾗ ἱππεὺς εἶ ἢ ᾗ κιθαριστής; τί ἄν μοι ἀπεκρίνω;

ΙΩΝ. Ἧι ἱππεύς, ἔγωγ' ἄν.

ΣΩ. Οὐκοῦν εἰ καὶ τοὺς εὖ κιθαρίζοντας διε- 10 γίγνωσκες, ὡμολόγεις ἄν, ᾗ κιθαριστὴς εἶ, ταύτῃ διαγιγνώσκειν, ἀλλ' οὐχ ᾗ ἱππεύς.

ΙΩΝ. Ναί.

ΣΩ. Ἐπειδὴ δὲ τὰ στρατιωτικὰ γιγνώσκεις, πότερον ᾗ στρατηγικὸς εἶ γιγνώσκεις ἢ ᾗ ῥαψῳδὸς 15 ἀγαθός;

ΙΩΝ. Οὐδὲν ἔμοιγε δοκεῖ διαφέρειν.

541 ΣΩ. Πῶς; οὐδὲν λέγεις διαφέρειν; μίαν λέγεις τέχνην εἶναι τὴν ῥαψῳδικὴν καὶ τὴν στρατηγικὴν ἢ δύο; 20

ΙΩΝ. Μία ἔμοιγε δοκεῖ.

ΣΩ. Ὅστις ἄρα ἀγαθὸς ῥαψῳδός ἐστιν, οὗτος καὶ ἀγαθὸς στρατηγὸς τυγχάνει ὤν;

ΙΩΝ. Μάλιστα, ὦ Σώκρατες.

ΣΩ. Οὐκοῦν καὶ ὅστις ἀγαθὸς στρατηγὸς τυγχ- 25 άνει ὤν, ἀγαθὸς καὶ ῥαψῳδός ἐστιν.

ΙΩΝ. Οὐκ αὖ μοι δοκεῖ τοῦτο.

1 ἂν Sydenham; ἄρ' T: ἄρ' W: om. F | ἔγωγε F: ἐγὼ TW
8 ἀπεκρίνω F: ἀπεκρίνου TW

ΣΩ. Ἀλλ' ἐκεῖνο μὴν δοκεῖ σοι, ὅστις γε ἀγαθὸς
ῥαψῳδός, καὶ στρατηγὸς ἀγαθὸς εἶναι;   B
ΙΩΝ. Πάνυ γε.
ΣΩ. Οὐκοῦν σὺ τῶν Ἑλλήνων ἄριστος ῥαψῳδὸς
5 εἶ;
ΙΩΝ. Πολύ γε, ὦ Σώκρατες.
ΣΩ. Ἦ καὶ στρατηγός, ὦ Ἴων, τῶν Ἑλλήνων
ἄριστος εἶ;
ΙΩΝ. Εὖ ἴσθι, ὦ Σώκρατες· καὶ ταῦτά γε ἐκ
10 τῶν Ὁμήρου μαθών.
XII. ΣΩ. Τί δή ποτ' οὖν πρὸς τῶν θεῶν, ὦ
Ἴων, ἀμφότερα ἄριστος ὢν τῶν Ἑλλήνων, καὶ
στρατηγὸς καὶ ῥαψῳδός, ῥαψῳδεῖς μὲν περιιὼν τοῖς
Ἕλλησι, στρατηγεῖς δ' οὔ; ἢ ῥαψῳδοῦ μὲν δοκεῖ σοι C
15 χρυσῷ στεφάνῳ ἐστεφανωμένου πολλὴ χρεία εἶναι
τοῖς Ἕλλησι, στρατηγοῦ δὲ οὐδεμία;
ΙΩΝ. Ἡ μὲν γὰρ ἡμετέρα, ὦ Σώκρατες, πόλις
ἄρχεται ὑπὸ ὑμῶν καὶ στρατηγεῖται καὶ οὐδὲν δεῖται
στρατηγοῦ, ἡ δὲ ὑμετέρα καὶ ἡ Λακεδαιμονίων οὐκ ἄν
20 με ἕλοιτο στρατηγόν· αὐτοὶ γὰρ οἴεσθε ἱκανοὶ εἶναι.
ΣΩ. Ὦ βέλτιστε Ἴων, Ἀπολλόδωρον οὐ γιγνώσκεις τὸν Κυζικηνόν;
ΙΩΝ. Ποῖον τοῦτον;
ΣΩ. Ὃν Ἀθηναῖοι πολλάκις ἑαυτῶν στρατηγὸν
25 ᾕρηνται ξένον ὄντα· καὶ Φανοσθένη τὸν Ἄνδριον καὶ D
Ἡρακλείδην τὸν Κλαζομένιον, οὓς ἥδε ἡ πόλις ξένους
ὄντας, ἐνδειξαμένους ὅτι ἄξιοι λόγου εἰσί, καὶ εἰς
στρατηγίας καὶ εἰς τὰς ἄλλας ἀρχὰς ἄγει· Ἴωνα δ'
ἄρα τὸν Ἐφέσιον οὐχ αἱρήσεται στρατηγὸν καὶ

1 μὴν F: μὲν TW

τιμήσει, ἐὰν δοκῇ ἄξιος λόγου εἶναι; τί δέ; οὐκ
'Αθηναῖοι μέν ἐστε οἱ 'Εφέσιοι τὸ ἀρχαῖον, καὶ ἡ
E "Εφεσος οὐδεμιᾶς ἐλάττων πόλεως; ἀλλὰ γὰρ σύ,
ὦ "Ιων, εἰ μὲν ἀληθῆ λέγεις, ὡς τέχνῃ καὶ ἐπιστήμῃ
οἷός τε εἶ "Ομηρον ἐπαινεῖν, ἀδικεῖς, ὅστις ἐμοὶ ὑπο- 5
σχόμενος, ὡς πολλὰ καὶ καλὰ περὶ 'Ομήρου ἐπίστα-
σαι, καὶ φάσκων ἐπιδείξειν ἐξαπατᾷς με καὶ πολλοῦ
δεῖς ἐπιδεῖξαι, ὅς γε οὐδὲ ἄττα ἐστὶ ταῦτα, περὶ ὧν
δεινὸς εἶ, ἐθέλεις εἰπεῖν, πάλαι ἐμοῦ λιπαροῦντος,
ἀλλ' ἀτεχνῶς ὥσπερ ὁ Πρωτεὺς παντοδαπὸς γίγνει 10
στρεφόμενος ἄνω καὶ κάτω, ἕως τελευτῶν διαφυγών
542 με στρατηγὸς ἀνεφάνης, ἵνα μὴ ἐπιδείξῃς ὡς δεινὸς
εἶ τὴν περὶ 'Ομήρου σοφίαν. εἰ μὲν οὖν τεχνικὸς ὤν,
ὅπερ νῦν δὴ ἔλεγον, περὶ 'Ομήρου ὑποσχόμενος
ἐπιδείξειν ἐξαπατᾷς με, ἄδικος εἶ· εἰ δὲ μὴ τεχνικὸς 15
εἶ, ἀλλὰ θείᾳ μοίρᾳ κατεχόμενος ἐξ 'Ομήρου μηδὲν
εἰδὼς πολλὰ καὶ καλὰ λέγεις περὶ τοῦ ποιητοῦ,
ὥσπερ ἐγὼ εἶπον περὶ σοῦ, οὐδὲν ἀδικεῖς. ἑλοῦ οὖν
πότερα βούλει νομίζεσθαι ὑπὸ ἡμῶν ἄδικος ἀνὴρ εἶναι
ἢ θεῖος.   20

ΙΩΝ. Πολὺ διαφέρει, ὦ Σώκρατες· πολὺ γὰρ
κάλλιον τὸ θεῖον νομίζεσθαι.

B   ΣΩ. Τοῦτο τοίνυν τὸ κάλλιον ὑπάρχει σοι παρ'
ἡμῖν, ὦ "Ιων, θεῖον εἶναι καὶ μὴ τεχνικὸν περὶ
'Ομήρου ἐπαινέτην.   25

8 δεῖ σ' TW : δ' εἰς F

NOTES

References are given to the School Grammar of Rutherford (R.).

530 A. τὸν Ἴωνα χαίρειν, sc. κελεύω. Cf. Theocr. XIV. 1 χαίρην πολλὰ τὸν ἄνδρα Θυώνιχον. χαῖρε is a salutation used both at meeting and parting. Cf. salve in Latin.

ἡμῖν ἐπιδεδήμηκας. Ethic Dative, 'have come to visit us.'

ἐξ Ἐφέσου explanatory of οἴκοθεν, 'from your home at Ephesus' —a famous city of Asia Minor in the valley of the Cayster.

ἐξ Ἐπιδαύρου ἐκ τῶν Ἀσκληπιείων. 'From the festival of Aesculapius at Epidaurus.' Cf. previous note. Epidaurus on the N.E. coast of Argolis opposite Aegina was a centre of the worship of Aesculapius, the god of the healing art. Athletic and musical contests were held there in his honour. Cf. Pind. *Isth.* VII. 74–5 ἐπεί νιν Ἀλκαθόου τ' ἀγὼν σὺν τύχᾳ ἐν Ἐπιδαύρῳ τε πρὶν ἔδεκτο νεότας.

καὶ ῥαψῳδῶν. Rhapsodes were professional reciters of the works of the poets. They carried a lyre as a symbol of their art ; possibly they played a few notes upon it at the beginning and end of their recitations. They also gave explanations of the meaning of the poet (cf. 530 C). καί = also.

ἠγωνίζου τι ἡμῖν...ἠγωνίσω. Observe the tenses, the imperfect regarding the contest from the point of view of its duration, the aorist from the point of view of its result. ἡμῖν Ethic Dative, marking the person interested in the action, = let me ask.

530 B. εὖ λέγεις = 'Bravo !'

ὅπως νικήσομεν. After verbs of striving, taking care, and the like, the sense is completed by ὅπως with the Future Indicative (negative μή). Sometimes the verb of striving is omitted and ὅπως with the Future used alone with the force of an imperative, 'Be sure that'; 'Mind that.'

καὶ τὰ Παναθήναια. Internal or Cognate Accusative. The great Panathenaic festival was celebrated every four years in honour of Athena. The procession to the temple of the goddess was represented by Pheidias on the frieze of the Parthenon. καί, *i.e.* as well as at Epidaurus.

τῆς τέχνης. Verbs denoting envy, admiration, and the like, take a Genitive of that to which the emotion is due.

τὸ σῶμα. R. § 77.

καλλίστοις in agreement with ὑμῖν which is suggested by ὑμῶν τῇ τέχνῃ.

530 C. μὴ γιγνώσκοντα. Conditional use of the participle, 'unless he knows.'

γοῦν. This particle is regularly employed to introduce the ground upon which a statement has been made or a position taken up. Cf. *infr.* 540 D γνοίην γοῦν ἂν ἔγωγε οἷα στρατηγὸν πρέπει εἰπεῖν. So in Aristophanes, *e.g. Frogs* 289 ΔΙ. ποῖόν τι; ΞΑ. δεινόν· παντοδαπὸν γοῦν γίγνεται.

Μητρόδωρος ὁ Λαμψακηνός. Metrodorus of Lampsacus, a city of Asia Minor at the northern end of the Hellespont, was a friend of Anaxagoras the philosopher and interpreted Homer allegorically, understanding the various deities to represent physical phenomena. He flourished in the 1st half of the 5th century B.C.

Στησίμβροτος ὁ Θάσιος. Stesimbrotus of Thasos, an island in the Aegaean off the coast of Thrace, flourished in the middle of the 5th century B.C. and wrote a work upon Homer. He is mentioned also by Xenophon.

Γλαύκων. Probably an Athenian, since no local adjective is attached to his name, and to be identified with the Glaucon of whom Aristotle speaks (*Poetics*, 1461 b 1) as condemning the hasty conclusions drawn by some commentators as to a poet's meaning.

530 CD. ὡς οὔτε Μητρόδωρος...ἐγώ. The sentence was begun apparently as a comparative one (ὡς=in such manner as) and the predicate would naturally be ἔσχεν εἰπεῖν simply = was able to speak. But to the verb εἰπεῖν is appended an object διανοίας and thus there is added a fresh comparison οὕτω πολλὰς καὶ καλὰς ὅσας ἐγώ. For the irregular construction of the sentence we may compare 534 AB. The irregularity might be removed either by reading, with

Mr H. Richards, ὥστ' for ὡς, or by taking the conjunction in a causal sense = since.

530 D.   εὖ λέγεις = 'I am glad to hear it.' Cf. supr. 530 B.

Ὁμηριδῶν.   The word Ὁμηρίδαι occurs elsewhere in Plato (*Rep.* 599 E; *Phaedr.* 252 B) always in the sense 'devotees of Homer.'   These Ὁμηρίδαι must not be confused with the clan in Chios mentioned by Strabo as bearing that name.

ἔτι ποιήσομαι σχολήν.   Observe that the Middle Voice (ποιεῖσθαι), not the Active (ποιεῖν), is used with a noun to form a periphrasis equivalent in meaning to a simple verb (*e.g.* here σχολάσω). 'Some day I shall take an opportunity.'

τοσόνδε.   As a rule τοσοῦτος refers to what has preceded, τοσόσδε to what follows.

531 A.   Ὁμήρου.   Homer is the name given to the putative author of the *Iliad* and the *Odyssey*.   Other works too were attributed to him in antiquity such as the *Thebais* (Paus. IX. 9. 5), the *Cypria* and the *Epigoni* (Herod. II. 117; IV. 32).   Of Homer nothing is known.   It is probable that the *Iliad* and the *Odyssey* as we have them are not the original work of a single man but have undergone a process of interpolation, alteration, and addition at the hands of several poets.

Ἡσιόδου.   Hesiod was a Boeotian poet of early but uncertain date.   The chief works attributed to him are (i) Ἔργα καὶ Ἡμέραι, (ii) Θεογονία, (iii) Ἀσπὶς Ἡρακλέους, (iv) ἢ οἷαι.   The last of these has not come down to us.

Ἀρχιλόχου.   Archilochus, a lyric poet belonging to the island of Paros, flourished in the 1st half of the 7th century B.C.   He is credited with the invention of the iambic line and the most striking characteristic of his verse was its trenchant vigour (cf. Horace, *A. P.* 79 Archilochum proprio rabies armavit iambo).   Fragments only of his poetry are extant.

531 B.   ὧν πέρι μὴ ταὐτὰ λέγουσιν;   If the relative pronoun introducing a clause has an indefinite antecedent, the clause is negatived by μή, not οὐ.

531 C.   ποτέ emphasising the question = 'pray.'   Cf. tandem in Latin.

ἰδιωτῶν καὶ δημιουργῶν, *i.e.* men with and without special professions.   For ἰδιώτης cf. note on 532 D.

περὶ θεῶν...ὁμιλούντων, ὡς ὁμιλοῦσι. Not infrequently the subject of a subordinate clause is introduced by anticipation in the sentence upon which that subordinate clause depends—sometimes as the direct object of the verb, sometimes in the genitive case governed by the preposition περί. Cf. inf. 531 E. R. §§ 250–1.

γενέσεις. The Accusative case here replaces περί with the Genitive.

531 D. ἄμεινον μέντοι νὴ Δία. Both μέντοι and νὴ Δία emphasize the adverb ἄμεινον.

ὦ φίλε κεφαλή. So 'carum caput' is used in Latin. Cf. Verg. *Aen.* IV. 354; Hor. *Carm.* I. 24. 2.

531 E. περὶ ὑγιεινῶν σιτίων ὁποῖά ἐστιν. R. § 250.

τὸν ἄριστα λέγοντα γνώσεται ὅτι ἄριστα λέγει. R. § 244. Cf. infr. 533 C.

ἐν κεφαλαίῳ = ad summam, 'briefly,' 'in a word.'

532 A. οὐδὲ τὸν εὖ, sc. λέγοντα γνώσεται. Observe the force of οὐδέ; 'will not know the man who speaks well *either*,' *i.e.* any more than he will know the man who speaks ill.

532 B. τί οὖν ποτὲ τὸ αἴτιον. For the use of ποτέ in a question, vid. *sup.* 531 C.

ὅταν μέν τις...διαλέγηται...ἐπειδὰν δέ τις...μνησθῇ. Notice the change of conjunction and tense: 'when a man is talking...after he has mentioned.'

532 C. εὐπορῶ ὅτι λέγω. λέγω is pres. subj. in an indirect deliberative question. R. § 247.

ποιητικὴ γάρ πού ἐστι τὸ ὅλον. Notice the emphatic position of τὸ ὅλον. 'Surely it is the whole that is poetry.' By τὸ ὅλον is meant the whole which includes every part of poetic activity, the work of Hesiod, Archilochus, and the rest, as well as that of Homer. Cf. infr. 532 E γραφικὴ γάρ τίς ἐστι τέχνη τὸ ὅλον; 'It is the whole that we may call (τις) the art of painting?'

532 D. ὅλην emphatic, 'in its entirety.'

ὁ αὐτὸς τρόπος τῆς σκέψεώς ἐστι περὶ ἁπασῶν τῶν τεχνῶν. In effect, περὶ ἁπασῶν τῶν τεχνῶν repeats the force of ἡντινοῦν in the subordinate clause. 'After a man has acquired any other art whatsoever in its entirety, in the case of every art, there is the same method of enquiry,' sc. in regard to both the good and the bad in that art.

ὧν ὑμεῖς ᾄδετε τὰ ποιήματα, *i.e.* the poets.

ἰδιώτην ἄνθρωπον. The rhapsode is a professional character, Socrates only an amateur, without special training. Cf. *Soph.* 221 C ἰδιώτην ἤ τινα τέχνην ἔχοντα θετέον εἶναι τὸν ἀσπαλιευτήν: *supr.* 531 C.

532 E. καὶ περὶ τούτου οὗ νῦν ἠρόμην σε. The Relative is attracted into the case of the antecedent. καί = for instance.

παντὸς ἀνδρός = 'in the power of any man.' Genitive of Possession, R. § 106 (2). Cf. Dem. *Olynth.* I. 16, τὸ μὲν οὖν ἐπιτιμᾶν ἴσως φῆσαί τις ἂν ῥᾴδιον καὶ παντὸς εἶναι.

λάβωμεν γὰρ τῷ λόγῳ = (lit.) 'let us apprehend it with the argument'; *i.e.* 'let us argue it out.'

γραφικὴ γάρ τίς ἐστι. The details of a discussion are regularly introduced by γάρ.

καὶ γραφεῖς = painters as well, *i.e.* as an art of painting.

Πολυγνώτου. The celebrated painter Polygnotus flourished in the middle of the 5th century B.C. A native of Thasos he received the citizenship of Athens where his chief works were to be found in the Temple of Theseus, the Anaceum, the Stoa Poikilé and the Propylaea. He also exercised his art to adorn the temple of Apollo at Delphi. His subjects were generally drawn from Homer and other poets of the Epic Cycle.

ἀποφαίνειν. Epexegetic or Explanatory Infinitive defining the activity in which skill (δεινός) is exhibited.

ἃ εὖ τε γράφει καὶ ἃ μή. We should have expected rather ἅ τε εὖ γράφει, as infr. 533 C ἅ τε εὖ ῥαψῳδεῖ καὶ ἃ μή. For the negative μή cf. *supr.* 531 B.

533 A. οὐκ ἔχει ὅ τι συμβάληται. For the mood of συμβάληται cf. 532 C εὐπορῶ ὅτι λέγω.

ὅτου βούλει. The relative pronoun is attracted into the case of its antecedent. Cf. supr. 532 E οὗ...ἠρόμην.

εὐπορεῖ ὅ τι εἴπῃ. Vid. *supr.* 532 C.

Δαιδάλου τοῦ Μητίονος. Daedalus is a mythical character, the personification of skill in working in wood and stone; hence his name, Cunning the son of Craft. The legend relates that he was an Athenian, who jealous of his nephew's superior skill murdered him. Condemned to death by the Areopagus he fled to Crete where he won the friendship of Minos. He fashioned the labyrinth in which the Minotaur was kept, but incurring the hostility of Minos fled from his wrath on wings constructed by himself. According to one version of the story he first descended to Earth at Cumae in Italy and dedicated there his wings. (Verg. *Aen.* VI. 14 ff.)

'Επειοῦ τοῦ Πανοπέως. Epeus with the help of Athena built the wooden horse by means of which Troy was captured. Cf. Hom. *Od.* VIII. 493 ἵππου κόσμον ἄεισον | δουρατέου τὸν 'Επειὸς ἐποίησεν σὺν 'Αθήνῃ; Verg. *Aen.* II. 264.

Θεοδώρου τοῦ Σαμίου. Two famous Samian artists bore the name Theodorus. The first was the son of Rhoecus and brother of Telecles, a statuary in bronze and sculptor in wood as well as an architect. He was engaged in the construction of the famous temples of Hera at Samos and Artemis at Ephesus. In conjunction with Telecles he made the wooden statue of Apollo Pythius for the Samians. He flourished circ. 600 B.C. The second Theodorus was the nephew of the first, being son to Telecles. He was a distinguished statuary in bronze and an engraver on metals and jewels. He practised his art during the earlier half of the 6th century B.C.

533 B. οὐκ ἔχων ὅ τι εἴπῃ. Cf. *supr.* 533 A οὐκ ἔχει ὅτι συμβάληται.

οὐδ' ἐν αὐλήσει γε οὐδὲ ἐν κιθαρίσει οὐδὲ ἐν κιθαρῳδίᾳ οὐδὲ ἐν ῥαψῳδίᾳ. Observe the repeated οὐδέ. 'No, nor in flute playing, nor again in playing the lyre, nor in singing to it either, nor yet in rhapsody, have you ever seen,' et cet.

'Ολύμπου. Olympus was a mythical Mysian flute player belonging to the Mysian and Phrygian school of music, the chief figure in which was Marsyas whose pupil Olympus is sometimes said to have been.

Θαμύρου. Thamyras was a celebrated Thracian lyrist who challenged the Muses to a contest and was struck with blindness for his presumption. He is represented in art with a broken lyre in his hand. Cf. (Eurip.) *Rhesus* 925 (the Muse is speaking) Θάμυριν ὃς ἡμῶν πόλλ' ἐδέννασεν τέχνην; Hom. *Il.* II. 595.

533 C. 'Ορφέως. Like Thamyras, Orpheus was a famous Thracian lyrist. So great was the power of his music that it drew rocks and trees after him (cf. Verg. *Eclog.* III. 46 Orpheaque in medio posuit *silvasque sequentes*), tamed the wild beasts, and even

overcame the most inexorable of deities, Hades. (Verg. *Georg.* IV.
455 ff.)

Φημίου. Phemius was a minstrel who was constrained to sing
for the pleasure of the suitors in the hall of Odysseus in Ithaca.
Cf. Hom. *Od.* XVIII. 331.

Ἴωνος. Nothing is known of Ion beyond what we learn in this
dialogue.

καίτοι ὅρα τοῦτο τί ἐστιν = lit. 'And yet do you look at this,
what it is,' *i.e.* 'However, look what this is.' For the subject of
the subordinate clause made the object of the verb of the principal
clause, cf. *supr.* 531 E, τὸν ἄριστα λέγοντα γνώσεται ὅτι ἄριστα λέγει.
τοῦτο = τὸ ἐμὲ περὶ Ὁμήρου κάλλιστ' ἀνθρώπων λέγειν καὶ εὐπορεῖν.

ἔρχομαί γέ σοι ἀποφαινόμενος. In Herodotus and in Plato
ἔρχομαι is used with the Future participle in the sense, 'I intend to,'
'I am about to.' But in Plato, *Phaedo* 100 B (ἔρχομαι ἐπιχειρῶν
σοι ἐπιδείξασθαι) and here it is used with the present participle in
the same meaning. Similarly μέλλειν is followed both by the present
and by the future infinitive.

533 D. **γάρ** serves to introduce the detailed explanation. Cf.
supr. 532 E.

οὐκ ὂν παρὰ σοί = (lit.) 'it not being in *your* power' (Latin
apud te). Accusative Absolute, R. § 366. In the MSS. the letters
οὐ appear to have been written once instead of twice, a mistake
technically known as haplography. Some, however, accept the
reading of the MSS. and assume that the use of a periphrastic form,
made up of the participle of a verb and εἶναι in place of the
simple verb (*e.g.* 530 B πρέπον εἶναι = πρέπειν), is here extended to
the substantive verb itself, so that ἐστι...οὐκ ὂν = οὐκ ἔστι.

ὃ νῦν δὴ ἔλεγον. *Supr.* 532 C.

ὥσπερ ἐν τῇ λίθῳ, sc. δύναμίς ἐστι. λίθος is feminine in gender
only when it refers to a special kind of stone, *e.g.* ἡ διαφανὴς
λίθος = crystal.

Εὐριπίδης. Euripides, one of the three great Attic tragedians,
flourished in the latter half of the 5th century B.C., the dates
traditionally assigned for his birth and death being 480 B.C. and
406 B.C. He was a friend of Anaxagoras, the philosopher, and
keenly interested in physical enquiry. Cf. *e.g.* frag. 271.

Μαγνῆτις = of Magnesia, a town in Caria near the river

Maeander. Pliny (*N. H.* XXXVI. 127), citing as his authority for the statement Nicander, declares that the stone was so called from the name of its discoverer, Magnes.

Ἡρακλείαν= of Heraclea, a town in Caria some 25 miles south of Magnesia. But popularly, no doubt, the adjective was under-stood to connect the stone owing to its power of attraction directly with Heracles, the embodiment of physical force.

ὥστε δύνασθαι...ὥστ' ἐνίοτε ὁρμαθὸς...ἤρτηται. Notice the variation of mood. With the infinitive ὥστε introduces a result closely connected with and subordinated to the action of the clause, upon which the ὥστε clause depends; with the indicative ὥστε introduces what is in effect an independent sentence.

533 E. ὁρμαθὸς ἐξαρτᾶται. Contrast the tense of ἐξαρτᾶται with ἤρτηται above. 'A hanging string is formed' > < 'A string hangs suspended.'

534 A. καὶ οἱ μελοποιοί. The subject is repeated after the intervening ὥσπερ clause. καί is added in reference to the other members of the comparison, viz. οἱ κορυβαντιῶντες.

εἰς τὴν ἁρμονίαν καὶ εἰς τὸν ῥυθμόν. A harmony is a com-bination of notes. Rhythm depends upon the order in which stressed and unstressed syllables are arranged.

καὶ κατεχόμενοι...ἡ ψυχὴ τοῦτο ἐργάζεται. κατεχόμενοι agrees with οἱ μελοποιοί, which was intended to serve as the subject to the verb. But after the intervening ὥσπερ clause the form of the subject is changed to τῶν μελοποιῶν ἡ ψυχή, and the participle κατεχόμενοι is left without any grammatical construction.

ὅπερ αὐτοὶ λέγουσι. The antecedent to the relative pronoun is not τοῦτο but the whole sentence τῶν μελοποιῶν ἡ ψυχὴ τοῦτο ἐργάζεται.

λέγουσι γὰρ δήπουθεν κ.τ.λ. Cf. *e.g.* Pind. *Ol.* IX. 40–1; *Pyth.* VI. 1–2; Bacchylides IX. 10; Aristoph. *Birds* 748 f.; Leonidas of Tarentum, *Anthol.* I. 1; Horace *Carm.* IV. 2. 28 f.

534 B. ἅτε οὖν οὐ τέχνῃ ποιοῦντες...λέγοντες. These participles suggest that a plural subject will follow, instead of which ἕκαστος, grammatically singular, is substituted. Cf. *supr.* 534 A.

ὥσπερ σὺ περὶ Ὁμήρου, sc. πολλὰ λέγεις καὶ καλά.

534 C. διθυράμβους. The dithyramb was a form of poetry orgiastic in character and probably of Eastern origin. It is first

mentioned in a fragment of Archilochus (vid. *supr.* 531 A) who says that he knows well how to lead off the dithyramb when his brain is smitten with wine as with a thunderbolt. It was greatly advanced by Arion of Lesbos (circ. 600 B.C.) who is thus sometimes called its inventor. He apparently organised and trained choruses to sing it and is said to have given to it a more 'tragic' tone. This may mean that he restrained the extravagance of the dance by which it was accompanied. It was from the dithyramb that, according to Aristotle (*Poet.* I. 4), Greek tragedy took its rise.

ἐγκωμία. These were laudatory odes. Pindar wrote many such.

ὑπορχήματα. These were choral hymns, resembling paeans, sung with dance and gesture and written mostly in cretics (- ⌣ -). Fragments of ὑπορχήματα are extant composed by Pindar, Simonides and Bacchylides.

ἔπη. Poems in hexameter verse, heroic or didactic, such as Homer's *Iliad* and Hesiod's *Works and Days*.

ἰάμβους. Such verses as those of Archilochus, vid. *sup.* 531 A.

τὰ δ' ἄλλα φαῦλος. Accusative of Respect, R. § 79.

τούτοις χρῆται ὑπηρέταις. Observe ὑπηρέταις, used predicatively without the article, = 'as servants.' Cf. *infr.* 537 C τέχνην ταύτην ἔχει.

534 D. οἷς νοῦς μὴ πάρεστιν. For the negative cf. *sup.* 531 B.

Τύννιχος ὁ Χαλκιδεύς. Tynnichus is only a name to us. We hear of him in a story told of Aeschylus, which relates that the latter refused to write a paean, a choral hymn of thanksgiving and praise proper to Apollo, on the ground that the paean of Tynnichus, like an ancient statue, possessed a venerable sanctity which no new work could hope to rival. Chalcis was a city of Euboea so called from the copper mines (χαλκός) near it.

ἀτεχνῶς (to be distinguished by its accent from ἀτέχνως = un-skilfully) = 'exactly,' 'precisely,' and modifies the clause ὅπερ αὐτὸς (*i.e.* Τύννιχος) λέγει. Cf. *supr.* 532 C ἀτεχνῶς νυστάζω = 'I simply nod.'

ὅπερ αὐτὸς λέγει. The antecedent to the relative is the phrase εὕρημά τι Μοισᾶν, not εὕρημά τι alone.

Μοισᾶν = Μουσῶν. The form is due to the fact that the phrase is a quotation from Tynnichus. Cf. *infr.* 535 B.

535 A. ἅπτει...τῆς ψυχῆς. Verbs of Touching are followed by the Genitive. R. § 112.

535 B. ὅ τι ἄν σε ἔρωμαι. For the double Accusative cf. R. § 66.

τοὺς θεωμένους. Observe that this word which means strictly 'spectators' comes to be used generally for 'audience.'

τὸν 'Οδυσσέα κ.τ.λ. Hom. *Od.* XXII. 2 ff.

οὐδόν. This is the Homeric form which is preserved in the reminiscence of the passage in the poet. Cf. *supr.* 534 E.

'Αχιλλέα ἐπὶ τὸν "Εκτορα ὁρμῶντα. Hom. *Il.* XXII. 131 ff.

τῶν περὶ 'Ανδρομάχην ἐλεινῶν τι. Hom. *Il.* VI. 390 ff.; XXIV. 725 ff.

ἥ περὶ 'Εκάβην. Hom. *Il.* XXII. 79 ff.; XXIV. 748 ff.

ἥ περὶ Πρίαμον. Hom. *Il.* XXII. 33 ff.; XXIV. 477 ff.

πότερον ἔμφρων εἶ ἥ ἔξω σαυτοῦ γίγνει. The idea that the poet when engaged in composition is no longer himself but is possessed by an alien power—an idea here extended to apply to the rhapsode —is found in Plato also in *Phaedrus* 245 A; *Apology* 22 B; *Meno* 99 C; *Laws* 719 C. Compare Aristotle's division of poets into εὐφυεῖς and μανικοί, the latter being further defined as ἐκστατικοί (Aristot. *Poet.* 1455 a 32). The thought has reappeared in modern literature, *e.g.* in Shakespeare, *Midsummer Night's Dream*, Act V. Sc. 1:—

'The poet's eye in a fine frenzy rolling
   Doth glance from heaven to earth, from earth to heaven.'

535 C. οἷς λέγεις. The Relative is attracted into the case of its antecedent. Cf. *supr.* 532 E, R. § 41.

'Ιθάκη. Ithaca, an island off the coast of Acarnania to the west of Greece, was the home of Odysseus.

Τροία. Troy was a district in the north west of Asia Minor. Its chief city was Ilium, the capital of Priam, which was taken and sacked by the Greeks after a siege of ten years. Its site has been identified with the modern Hissarlik where important archaeological discoveries have been made.

δακρύων ἐμπίμπλανται. Words denoting fullness and the reverse are followed by the Genitive Case. R. § 113.

ὀρθαὶ αἱ τρίχες ἵστανται. Observe the tense and the position of the adjective = 'rises on end.'

ὑπὸ φόβου. ὑπό is employed with the Genitive to denote cause especially with words denoting feelings, which may be thus easily personified.

535 D. κλάῃ τε…ἢ φοβῆται. For ἤ answering to τε cf. *Theaetetus* 143 C αἱ μεταξὺ τῶν λόγων διηγήσεις περὶ αὐτοῦ τε…ἢ αὖ περὶ τοῦ ἀποκρινομένου.

πλέον ἤ ἐν δισμυρίοις ἀνθρώποις. So in Xenophon, *Oec.* 21. 3 πλέον ἤ ἐν διπλασίῳ χρόνῳ='in more than twice the time.' The number appears to represent a rough estimate of the adult free male population of Athens at that time.

οὐ πάνυ='Not altogether,' and so, by the figure of speech called Litotes or Understatement, it becomes equivalent to a very decided negative, 'Assuredly not'; 'By no means.'

ὥς γε τἀληθὲς εἰρῆσθαι. The Infinitive with ὡς is often used absolutely with a limiting or defining force. Cf. ὡς ἔπος εἰπεῖν='so to say'; ὡς συνελόντι εἰπεῖν='to speak concisely.' R. § 340.

τῶν θεατῶν τοὺς πολλοὺς ταὐτὰ ταῦτα ἐργάζεσθε. Vide for the double Accusative R. § 74; for the position of the Genitive R. § 102. Cf. 530 A τὰ πρῶτα τῶν ἄθλων. ὑμεῖς=you rhapsodists.

535 E. δεινὸν ἐμβλέποντας. Adverbial Accusative. R. § 72 (3). **καθίσω**=exactly the English, 'set.'

ὧν ἐγὼ ἔλεγον. Cf. on *supr.* 532 E περὶ τούτου οὗ νῦν ἠρόμην.

536 A. ἀνακρεμαννὺς ἐξ ἀλλήλων τὴν δύναμιν. Cf. 535 E ἀπ᾽ ἀλλήλων τὴν δύναμιν λαμβάνειν. Strictly these phrases should express the mutual reaction of A on B and B on A. But they are applied to denote the repetition of an action in a fresh direction, as the meaning evidently is that the magnetic power passes from A to B and from B *to* C, not that it passes back again from B to A.

ἐκ πλαγίου…δακτυλίων, 'suspended sideways from the rings that hang from the Muse.'

536 AB. καὶ ὁ μὲν τῶν ποιητῶν…ἔχεται γάρ. 'And one of the poets is in dependence on one Muse, another on another. We use the expression "is in the possession of." But it is the same thing. For he is in her grasp.'

αὐτό=ἐξήρτηται. Observe the article τό used as a pronoun. Cf. 537 A τοῖιν.

536 B. Ὀρφέως. Vide *supr.* 533 C.

Μουσαίου. Musaeus, a mythological personage, was associated in some legends with Orpheus, whose son he is said to have been. Several poetical compositions and a number of oracles were attributed to him. Other legends connect him with the famous family of the Eumolpidae and the worship of Demeter at Eleusis.

ἐπειδὰν μέν τις ἄλλου του ποιητοῦ ᾄδῃ. Sc. μέλος which is inserted in the corresponding clause below.

εὐπορεῖς ὅ τι λέγῃς. Cf. *supr.* 532 C.

536 C. τοῦ θεοῦ. Possessive Genitive. R. 106 (2).

σχημάτων καὶ ῥημάτων. Notice the verbal jingle. So in Aristoph. *Frogs* 463 τὸ σχῆμα καὶ τὸ λῆμ᾽ ἔχων. For the Genitive Case cf. *supr.* 535 C; R. § 113.

τῶν δὲ ἄλλων οὐ ᾽φροντίζουσιν. Verbs denoting 'care for' and 'neglect' are followed by the Genitive Case. Cf. R. § 100 (3).

ὅ μ᾽ ἐρωτᾷς. Cf. *supr.* 533 C, 532 B. For the double Accusative cf. 535 B.

536 D. οἶμαι οὐδ᾽ ἂν σοὶ δόξαιμι. οἶμαι is parenthetic = 'methinks.' Observe οὐδὲ σοί = 'to you either' (*i.e.* any more than to myself).

536 E. ὧν ῞Ομηρος λέγει. The relative is attracted into the case of the suppressed antecedent. Cf. *supr.* 532 E, 535 E.

περὶ οὐδενὸς ὅτου οὔ = 'about everything.' R. § 44.

ὧν σὺ μὲν τυγχάνεις οὐκ εἰδώς. For the attraction of the relative cf. *supr.* ὧν ῞Ομηρος λέγει.

καὶ ταῦτα ποῖά ἐστιν. The question is an incredulous one, as generally when the interrogation is prefaced by καὶ. For the force of ποῖα cf. *infr.* 541 C.

537 A. ἃ λέγει Νέστωρ. Hom. *Il.* XXIII. 335 ff.

περὶ τὴν καμπήν, 'about the turn': 'the turn' formed the half-way point of the δίαυλος, the race out and in. Cf. Aesch. *Agam.* 344 κάμψαι διαύλου θάτερον κῶλον πάλιν.

τῇ ἱπποδρομίᾳ τῇ ἐπὶ Πατρόκλῳ = 'the chariot racing for (*i.e.* in honour of) Patroclus.'

κλινθῆναι δὲ κ.τ.λ. The quotation presents the following variations from the received text of Homer (i) κλινθῆναι δὲ καὶ αὐτός for αὐτὸς δὲ κλινθῆναι, (ii) ἐυξέστῳ for ἐυπλέκτῳ.

κλινθῆναι. Infinitive used with the force of an Imperative. So below, κέντσαι, εἶξαι, and ἀλέασθαι.

ἧκ᾽ ἐπ᾽ ἀριστερὰ τοῖιν = 'slightly to the left of them' (*i.e.* the horses). Observe the Epic form τοῖιν for τοῖν, the article being used in Homer as a pronoun.

537 B. πλήμνη κύκλου ποιητοῖο = 'the nave of the wrought wheel.'

δοάσσεται. Subjunctive Mood.

λίθον. For the case cf. *supr.* 535 A ἅπτει...τῆς ψυχῆς.

537 C. εἴτε ὀρθῶς λέγει...εἴτε μή. Sc. ὀρθῶς. In indirect questions introduced by εἰ (=whether) μή may be used as well as οὔ.

πότερον ὅτι τέχνην ταύτην ἔχει. τέχνην is used predicatively and hence there is no article. 'Because he has this as an art,' *i.e.* 'because this is his art.' For the attraction of ταύτην into the gender of τέχνην cf. R. § 51.

οὐκοῦν ἑκάστη τῶν τεχνῶν...γιγνώσκειν. Compare the argument *supr.* 531 B. There the mastery of a particular artist over a particular subject-matter was developed to shew that Ion's skill, if an art, should apply to all poets; here it is used to prove that Ion can know nothing of any poet. The contradiction is only apparent. Ion is ignorant of the scope and standards of criticism. Hence he is an equally incompetent critic of all poets and is further unable to distinguish the subject-matter of the art, to which he lays claim, from those of seamanship, medicine, strategy and the like.

537 D. τὴν μὲν ἑτέραν...τὴν δ' ἑτέραν. Observe that ἑτέραν is predicative. 'Do you say that one art is one and another another?'

ἆρα ὥσπερ ἐγὼ τεκμαιρόμενος, ὅταν...ἑτέρων, οὕτω καλῶ...οὕτω καὶ σύ; The first οὕτω sums up the ὅταν clause; the second οὕτω answers to ὥσπερ. 'Do you too judge as I do and when one art is mastery of one subject-matter and the other of another, in that case (οὕτω) call the one art one and the other different?'

537 E. ὁπότε γε—εἴη = 'inasmuch as it would be possible.' For the mood cf. R. § 299.

538 B. περὶ τῶν ἐπῶν ὧν εἶπες. Cf. *supr.* 536 E.

εἴτε καλῶς λέγει εἴτε μή. Cf. *supr.* 537 C.

ἑτέρα ἐστὶ τῆς ἡνιοχικῆς. For ἕτερος followed by the Genitive Case cf. *infr.* 540 A; Thuc. I. 28 φίλους...ἑτέρους τῶν νῦν ὄντων; R. § 133.

538 C. τῷ Μαχάονι. Machaon, a son of Aesculapius, with his brother Podaleirius led thirty ships with men from Tricca, Ithome and Oechalia to assist Agamemnon against Troy. He acted as surgeon to the Greek forces and was wounded by Paris but rescued by Nestor.

Ἑκαμήδη. Hecamede, daughter of Arsinous, king of Tenedos, was assigned, when Achilles sacked that island, to Nestor 'for that he was foremost of all in counsel' (*Il.* XI. 627).

καὶ λέγει πως οὕτως. The quotation is made up from three lines, viz. *Il.* XI. 639-40 (οἴνῳ...χαλκείῃ) and *ibid.* 630 with substitution of παρά for ἐπί. φησίν is of course parenthetic (=inquit) as *supr.* 537 A.

οἴνῳ Πραμνείῳ. Pramnian wine was a rough, strong brand, so called according to the Ancient Scholiasts from a Mount Pramné which was placed by them in various localities.

κνῆ. Epic Aorist, κνάω='I scrape,' 'I grate.'

εἴτε ὀρθῶς λέγει εἴτε μή. Cf. on *supr.* 537 C.

ἰατρικῆς...ῥαψῳδικῆς. Sc. τέχνης. For the Genitive Case cf. 532 E, R. § 106 (2).

538 D. ἡ δὲ μολυβδαίνη κ.τ.λ. The quotation is from *Il.* XXIV. 80-2 describing the descent of Iris from Olympus by command of Zeus in search of Thetis. The variations from the received text of Homer are (i) ἵκανεν for ὄρουσεν, (ii) ἐμμεμαυῖα for ἐμβεβαυῖα, (iii) μετ' ἰχθύσι for ἐπ' ἰχθύσι, (iv) πῆμα for κῆρα.

ἐμμεμαυῖα. Perfect Participle, equivalent in force to an adverb, 'furiously.'

φῶμεν='Are we to say?' R. § 227.

ἁλιευτικῆς τέχνης...ῥαψῳδικῆς. Cf. *supr.* 538 C.

κρῖναι. Epexegetic or explanatory Infinitive, defining in what regard these verses belong to the art of the fisherman or the rhapsode. Cf. *supr.* 532 E.

σοῦ ἐρομένου, εἰ ἔροιό με. The hypothetical clause repeats in another form the force of the Genitive Absolute. 'When you ask me, if you were to do so.'

538 E. ἴθι μοι ἔξευρε καὶ κ.τ.λ. For μοι (=pray) cf. 530 A ἡμῖν. καὶ τὰ τοῦ μάντεως='also what belongs to the prophet,' *i.e.* in addition to the examples already given of what belongs to the fisherman, the physician and the chariot-driver.

πολλαχοῦ μὲν γὰρ καὶ ἐν Ὀδυσσείᾳ λέγει, answered below by πολλαχοῦ δὲ καὶ ἐν Ἰλιάδι.

οἷον καὶ ἃ κ.τ.λ. ='to take one example what' et cet.

ὁ τῶν Μελαμποδιδῶν μάντις Θεοκλύμενος. Melampus was according to the ancient tradition the first mortal who possessed prophetic powers. He was a dweller in Pylos but became a ruler of Argos (*Od.* XV. 225 ff.). Theoclymenus was a descendant of Melampus who inherited his prophetic gift. He had slain one of his kinsmen in Argos and had fled from vengeance to Pylos where he fell in with Telemachus who had gone thither to seek news of his father, Odysseus. Theoclymenus induced Telemachus to take him in his company back to Ithaca (_Od._ XV. 270 ff.).

539 A. δαιμόνιοι κ.τ.λ. The quotation is from _Od._ XX. 351-7 with the following variations from the received text of Homer; (i) δαιμόνιοι for ἇ δειλοί, (ii) γυῖα for γοῦνα, (iii) εἰδώλων τε for εἰδώλων δέ, (iv) l. 354 (αἵματι δ' ἐρράδαται τοῖχοι καλαί τε μεσόδμαι) is omitted.

τί κακὸν τόδε πάσχετε = 'What evil is this ye suffer?'

ὑμέων. Epic form = ὑμῶν.

εἰλύαται. Perf. Indic. Pass. 3rd pers. _plural_ of εἰλύω.

νέρθε τε γυῖα = 'And limbs beneath' (viz. your heads and faces).

539 B. οἷον καὶ ἐπὶ τειχομαχίᾳ· λέγει γὰρ καὶ ἐνταῦθα. For οἷον καὶ cf. _supr._ 538 E. For γάρ introducing the particular passage cited cf. _supr._ 532 E. The lines which follow are quoted from _Il._ XII. 200-7 with the substitution of (i) ἐγκάββαλ' for ἐνὶ κάββαλ', (ii) ἔπετο for πέτετο.

ἐπ' ἀριστερὰ λαὸν ἐέργων = 'skirting the host on his left' (lit. leftwards).

539 C. λήθετο...κόψε, sc. ὁ δράκων.

αὐτόν = τὸν αἰετόν.

ἔθεν. Epic form, here = ἑαυτοῦ.

539 D. καὶ σύ γε, ὦ Ἴων, ἀληθῆ ταῦτα λέγεις = 'And _you_, Ion, are right in saying so.' καὶ σύ γε implies 'you, no less than I.'

ἴθι δὴ καὶ σύ. For δή, used hortatively with the Imperative, cf. 538 D σκέψαι δή. καὶ σύ = 'you, in your turn.'

539 E. ἐπειδὴ καὶ ἐμπειρότερος εἶ ἐμοῦ. καί = 'further,' 'besides.' For the genitive of comparison ἐμοῦ cf. R. § 132.

τῶν Ὁμήρου. Adjectives denoting skill and lack of skill are followed by the Genitive Case.

ἐγὼ μέν φημι. The answering clause with δέ is left to be supplied (_e.g._ οἱ δὲ ἄλλοι ὅσα δή ποτέ φασι. 'I say everything, the rest as much as ever they do say.'). Thus μέν comes to be used to emphasize the pronoun = '_I_, Socrates, say everything.'

540 A. τῆς ἡνιοχικῆς, sc. τέχνης. For the case cf. 538 B.

οὐκοῦν καὶ ἑτέραν, κ.τ.λ. καί is to be taken with the whole clause = 'Then you admitted further that' et cet.

οὐδὲ ὁ ῥαψῳδός = 'nor the rhapsode either.' Cf. _supr._ 532 A.

πλήν γε ἴσως τὰ τοιαῦτα, sc. πάντα γνώσεται ὁ ῥαψῳδός.

540 B. τὰ τοιαῦτα δὲ λέγεις κ.τ.λ. τὰ τοιαῦτα is the object of the verb; the clause πλὴν...τεχνῶν is a completion of the predicate. "By 'such passages' you mean something like (σχεδόν τι) 'with the exception of what belongs to the other arts.'" We should have expected however rather πλὴν δὲ τὰ τοιαῦτα κ.τ.λ. but the expression is colloquially inexact. Cf. R. § 68.

540 C. οὐδὲ τοῦτο, sc. γνώσεται = 'he will not know this *either*,' *i.e.* any more than what a man in command should say in a tempest at sea.

ἀλλ' οὐχ ὁ βουκόλος = '*and* not the neatherd.' Observe that Greek uses the adversative, English the copulative conjunction.

540 D. τί δέ; = quid? Anglice, Oh!

γνοίην γοῦν ἂν ἔγωγε οἷα στρατηγὸν πρέπει εἰπεῖν. For the force of γοῦν cf. *supr.* 530 C. The pronoun is emphatic = 'At any rate I would know what it is fitting that a general should say.' Note the change from the Dative depending on πρέπει to the Accusative which is the subject of the dependent Infinitive.

ἴσως γὰρ εἶ καὶ στρατηγικός = 'Perhaps you have a talent for generalship too,' *i.e.* as well as for rhapsody.

καὶ γὰρ εἰ ἐτύγχανες ἱππικὸς ὤν, κ.τ.λ. For τυγχάνω with the participle cf. R. § 368. Observe the variation of tense through this and the following sentence. 'If you *were* skilled in horses (Imperfect), you would have known (Aorist) good and bad driving (viz. in the *past*, when you had your opportunity, *supr.* 538 B). But if I had asked you, what would you have answered?' (Both tenses Aorist referring to the past, viz. 538 B.)

ἱππαζομένους = 'driven' *not* 'ridden.'

ᾗ...ᾗ. Cf. Latin quâ...quâ.

οὐκοῦν εἰ καὶ τοὺς εὖ κιθαρίζοντας, κ.τ.λ. καί = 'again,' introducing a further example.

ἀλλ' οὐχ ᾗ ἱππεύς = '*and* not *qua* horseman.' Cf. *sup.* 540 C.

541 A. οὐκοῦν καὶ ὅστις ἀγαθὸς στρατηγὸς τυγχάνει ὤν, ἀγαθὸς καὶ ῥαψῳδός ἐστιν. The first καί (= 'further,' 'again') adds this proposition to the preceding converse one (ὅστις ἄρα ἀγαθὸς ῥαψῳδός ἐστιν, οὗτος καὶ ἀγαθὸς στρατηγὸς τυγχάνει ὤν); the second καί (= 'also,' 'too') marks the parallelism between ῥαψῳδός and στρατηγός.

ἐκεῖνο μήν. μήν, a strong form of μέν, emphasizes the pronoun. Cf. on *supr.* 539 E.

541 B. καὶ ταῦτά γε ἐκ τῶν Ὁμήρου μαθών. καὶ ταῦτα (cf. Latin idque) is used, generally with a participle, to add some circumstance upon which emphasis is laid. Cf. R. § 358.

τί δή ποτ' οὖν. Notice the accumulation of particles. 'Why then, pray, why.'

ἀμφότερα = 'in both respects.' Cf. *supr.* 534 C τὰ δ' ἄλλα φαῦλος: R. § 79.

541 C. ῥαψῳδοῦ...χρυσῷ στεφάνῳ ἐστεφανωμένου. For the splendid attire of the rhapsode cf. *supr.* 530 B; 535 D.

ἡ μὲν γὰρ ἡμετέρα...πόλις...ἡ δὲ ὑμετέρα, sc. Ephesus (*supr.* 530 A) and Athens. After the defeat of the Persian invasion in 478 B.C. a league was formed by the Greek states to protect them-selves, especially those of their number who dwelt on the east of the Aegaean sea, from the power of Persia. In the beginning no single state had suzerainty over the rest, but in the course of time the predominance and activity of Athens enabled her to reduce her fellow-members of the league to a position of dependence. In return for money contributions Athens undertook to equip and maintain a fleet and to suppress any Persian attempt at aggression. The money so obtained was used indeed to form a fleet, but that fleet was employed against recalcitrant allies. Thus cities like Ephesus ceased to have their own foreign policy and therefore no longer required generals.

οὐκ ἄν με ἕλοιτο στρατηγόν. For the double Accusative after αἱρεῖσθαι cf. *infr.* ὃν...στρατηγὸν ᾕρηνται; Ἴωνα δ' ἄρα...οὐχ αἱρήσεται στρατηγόν (541 D); R. § 68.

Ἀπολλόδωρον τὸν Κυζικηνόν. Cyzicus is a city situated on an island in the Propontis off the coast of Mysia, with which it was connected by a bridge and later by a mole, which has since become a considerable isthmus. Nothing is known of Apollodorus beyond what is stated here, viz. that he was a foreigner appointed by Athens to one of her military commands. This statement is repeated in Aelian (XIV. 5) who flourished in the latter half of the 3rd century A.D. Athenaeus (circ. 230 A.D.) refers (XI. p. 506) to this passage as an instance of Plato's 'malignity,' although no aspersion seems to be cast upon the generals mentioned who are simply instanced as foreigners taken by Athens into her service.

ποῖον τοῦτον; sc. οὐ γιγνώσκω = lit. 'what sort of a fellow (is) this (whom) I do not know?' ποῖος is frequently used in dialogue to refer contemptuously to some person or thing mentioned by a previous speaker. Cf. *supr.* 536 E: *Theaetetus* 180 B (Σωκράτης) ἀλλ', οἶμαι, τὰ τοιαῦτα τοῖς μαθηταῖς ἐπὶ σχολῆς φράζουσιν οὓς ἂν βούλωνται ὁμοίους αὐτοῖς ποιῆσαι. (Θεαίτητος) ποίοις μαθηταῖς, ὦ δαιμόνιε; So in Aristophanes, *Knights* 32. ποῖον βρέτας σύ γ'; *Clouds* 247; *Wasps* 1202. The question comes to be one in form only, the effect being to repeat derisively the expression of the previous speaker; so apparently here, ποῖον τοῦτον; = 'That fellow! Pooh!' The contemptuous tone is of course in keeping with Ion's character (vide Introd. p. xix) but may have given rise to the charge of 'malignity' referred to in the preceding note.

541 D. **καὶ Φανοσθένη τὸν ᾿Ανδριον καὶ ῾Ηρακλείδην τὸν Κλαζομένιον,** sc. οὐ γιγνώσκεις. Andros is one of the Cyclades, a group of islands in the Aegaean, south of Euboea and east of Attica. Phanosthenes is mentioned by Xenophon (*Hell.* I. 5. 18) as having been sent by the Athenians in the year 407–6 B.C. with four ships to replace Conon at Andros. Of Heracleides nothing is known. Clazomenae, a city of Asia Minor, was situated on the north side of the promontory formed by Mt Corycus which juts out into the Aegaean sea opposite the island of Chios.

῎Ιωνα δ' ἄρα τὸν ᾿Εφέσιον. ἄρα (observe the accent) is inferential = 'then.'

οὐκ ᾿Αθηναῖοι μέν ἐστε οἱ ᾿Εφέσιοι τὸ ἀρχαῖον καὶ ἡ ῎Εφεσος οὐδεμιᾶς ἐλάττων πόλεως; Observe that μέν is here answered by καί, antithesis passing into coordination. Cf. *sup.* 535 D where co-ordination (κλάῃ τε) passes into alternation (ἢ φοβῆται). τὸ ἀρχαῖον is an adverbial accusative defining the extent of the application of the verb (R. § 79). For the genitive of comparison πόλεως cf. 539 E ἐμοῦ.

Both Herodotus (I. 147. 2) and Thucydides (I. 2. 6) declare that the Ionian cities in Asia Minor, of which Ephesus was one, were settled as colonies from Athens. The former historian, however, maintains that the settlers included representatives of many peoples who had no claim to the name Ionian, while even the Athenians among them, who esteemed themselves the truest Ionians of all, took their wives from the Carians on whose lands they settled (Herod. I. 146. 4).

541 E. **ἀλλὰ γὰρ σύ, κ.τ.λ.** The conjunctions mark the trans-ition to the dilemma with which the dialogue concludes; 'But really.'

εἰ μὲν ἀληθῆ λέγεις...τὴν περὶ Ὁμήρου σοφίαν. This sentence is repeated in a shorter form in 542 A, εἰ μὲν οὖν...ἄδικος εἶ, and is, in this shortened form, contrasted with the sentence εἰ δὲ μὴ τεχνικὸς ...οὐδὲν ἀδικεῖς.

ὅστις...φάσκων ἐπιδείξειν ἐξαπατᾷς. Observe that the relative ὅστις imparts a causal force to the sentence = 'since you.' φάσκειν (cf. dictitare in Latin) is often used in the sense of saying *what is not true*, professing, pretending. The verb ἐπιδεικνύναι and the corresponding noun ἐπίδειξις are applied especially to a rhetorical display.

πολλοῦ δεῖς. Cf. R. § 130.

ὅς γε οὐδὲ ἅττα ἐστὶ ταῦτα...ἐθέλεις εἰπεῖν. The addition of γε to the relative pronoun confers upon it a causal force. So εἰ γε = since. Observe the force of οὐδέ : 'since you will not tell even what these subjects are,' sc. much less give an exhibition of your art (ἐπιδεικνύναι).

πάλαι ἐμοῦ λιπαροῦντος = 'although I have long been begging you.' πάλαι is used with the present tense to express an action begun in the past and still being continued. Cf. the use in Latin of iam pridem and in French of depuis longtemps.

ὁ Πρωτεύς. Proteus was a sea-god who possessed prophetic powers but would only display them if caught and held securely in spite of the diverse forms which he assumed. Cf. *Od.* IV. 455 ff.; Verg. *Georg.* IV. 440.

ἕως τελευτῶν...ἀνεφάνης. ἕως referring to a definite point in past time is followed by the Indicative Mood. τελευτῶν, the present participle of τελευτῶ (=lit. 'ending'), is used as the equivalent of an adverb 'at last.'

τὴν περὶ Ὁμήρου σοφίαν. Cf. *supr.* 534 C τὰ δ' ἄλλα φαῦλος, 541 B.

542 A. ὅπερ νῦν δὴ ἔλεγον = 'as I said just now,' *i.e. supr.* 541 E.

μηδὲν εἰδώς. The participle is concessive, 'although you know nothing,' 'without knowing.' Cf. *supr.* 535 D μηδὲν ἀπολωλεκώς.

κατεχόμενος ἐξ Ὁμήρου. For ἐκ with the Genitive of the agent cf. *supr.* 534 E; 536 B.

ὥσπερ ἐγὼ εἶπον περὶ σοῦ, viz. *supr.* 536 B–D.

APPENDIX I

The accounts of the life of Plato which have reached us are given in tabular form below. They are not of course to be regarded as necessarily possessing equal and independent authority.

(i) Apuleius (2nd century A.D.) prefixes a brief account of Plato's life to his work, *De Dogmate Platonis*.

(ii) Diogenes Laertius iii. contains a collection of facts about Plato derived from different sources and of unequal value.

(iii) Olympiodorus (6th century A.D.) gives in addition to a commentary on works of Plato an account of the philosopher's life.

(iv) A summary of Plato's life occurs in the lexicon known by the name of Suidas (? circ. 1000 A.D.).

(v) A similar summary is to be found in the work of Hesychius (? 4th century A.D.) which has included in it many interpolations and additions of later ages.

(vi) There is also extant an anonymous biography of uncertain but late date.

APPENDIX II

The following passages from Epicharmus will serve to illustrate the resemblance in style between the comic poet's writings and the dialogues of Plato.

(a) A. ἆρ᾽ ἔστιν αὔλησίς τι πρᾶγμα; B. πάνυ μὲν ὦν.

   A. ἄνθρωπος ὦν αὔλησίς ἐστιν; B. οὐδαμῶς.

   A. φέρ᾽ ἴδω, τί δ᾽ αὐλητάς; τίς εἶμέν τοι δοκεῖ;
   ἄνθρωπος ἢ οὐ γάρ; B. πάνυ μὲν ὦν. A. οὐκῶν δοκεῖ
   οὕτως ἔχειν τοι καὶ περὶ τώγαθοῦ; τό γα
   ἀγαθόν τι πρᾶγμ᾽ εἶμεν καθ᾽ αὑθ᾽· ὅστις δέ κα
   εἰδῇ μαθὼν τήν᾽, ἀγαθὸς ἤδη γίνεται.
   ὥσπερ γὰρ αἴ κ᾽ αὔλησιν αὐλητὰς μαθών,
   ἢ ὄρχησιν ὀρχηστάς τις ἢ πλοκεὺς πλοκάν,
   ἢ πᾶν γ᾽ ὁμοίως τῶν τοιούτων ὅτι τυ λῇς,
   οὐκ αὐτὸς εἴη χ᾽ ἁ τέχνα, τεχνικός γα μήν.

   (EPICHARMUS *apud* Diogenem Laertium, iii. 14.)

(b) A. οὐκ ἄρ᾽ ἔμολε πρᾶτον οὐδέν; B. οὐδὲ μὰ Δία δεύτερον
   τῶνδέ γ᾽ ὧν ἀμές νυν ὧδε λέγομες, ἀλλὰ τᾷδ᾽ ἔχει.
   αἴ ποτ᾽ ἀριθμόν τις περισσόν, αἰ δὲ λῇς, τὸν ἄρτιον
   ποτθέμεν λῇ ψῆφον, ἢ καὶ τᾶν ὑπαρχουσᾶν λαβεῖν,
   ἦ δοκεῖ κά τοι τόκ᾽ αὐτὸς εἶμεν; A. οὐκ ἐμὶν τάχα.

   B. οὐδὲ μὰν οὐδ᾽ αἰ ποτὶ μέτρον παχυαῖον ποτθέμεν
   λῇ τις ἅτερον μᾶκος, ἢ τοῦ πρόσθ᾽ ἐόντος ἀποταμεῖν,
   ἔτι χ᾽ ὑπάρχοι τῆνο τὸ μέτρον; A. οὐ γάρ. B. ὧδε νῦν ὅρη
   καὶ τὸς ἀνθρώπους· ὁ μὲν γὰρ αὔξεθ᾽, ὁ δέ γα μὰν φθίνει,
   ἐν μεταλλαγᾷ δὲ πάντες ἐντὶ πάντα τὸν χρόνον.
   ὃ δὲ μεταλλάσσει κατὰ φύσιν κωὔποκ᾽ ἐν τωὐτῷ μένει,
   ἅτερον εἴη κα τόδ᾽ ἤδη τοῦ παρεξεστακότος·
   καὶ τὺ δὴ κἠγὼ χθὲς ἄλλοι καὶ νῦν ἄλλοι τελέθομες,
   καὖθις ἄλλοι κωὔποκ᾽ αὐτοὶ τελέθομες καττὸν λόγον.

   (*Ibid.* iii. 12.)

INDEXES

I GRAMMATICAL AND GENERAL

II PROPER NAMES

Printed in the United States
by Bookmasters